INDOMITABLE

The Story of
Anthony Toomer Porter

Founder of Porter-Gaud School

Deborah Reinhold

Illustrations by Joanna Reinhold

HOME
HOUSE
PRESS

CHARLESTON, S.C.

Home House Press
109 Broad Street
Charleston, S.C.

To Lowry Coe, the very definition of "indomitable."

The events and people portrayed in this book are those chronicled in Anthony Toomer Porter's autobiography, *Led On! Step by Step: Life in the South, 1828-1898*, published by Home House Press. Dr. Porter's autobiography provides few details—so much of the description is the author's invention.

Some of the dialogue is taken directly from *Led On*—from Esther Porter to Miss Taylor, Charlotte to her family, Colonel Hagood and Dr. Porter to each other in the Battle of Secessionville, Cousin Laurens and Governor Aiken to Dr. Porter at Holy Communion, Lt. McQueen to Dr. Porter upon their reunion, General Sherman and Dr. Porter to each other, and Dr. Porter to the congregation in Brooklyn.

Acknowledgments

Several people encouraged me to complete *Indomitable* and offered their suggestions.

Many thanks to Joanna Reinhold for her insightful notes on the narrative and for her illustrations; to Beverly Stearns for her edits; to Tom Tisdale, Bob Reinhold, and Daniel Jordan for their encouragement; and to Forde Upshur for the title.

Chapter 1

A loud buzzing jolted Anthony from a deep sleep. He sat up, rubbed his eyes, and peered into the darkness of his room.

Buzzzt, Buzzt, buzzt.

Whatever was making the noise sounded angry. Anthony lay back in his bed, pulled the covers up over his ears, and tried to go back to sleep. Nothing doing.

Buzzt, buzzzzt, buzzzzzt.

Curious, Anthony threw back the covers, planted his feet on the floor, and felt on his bedside table for his candle and a match. Poof. The lit candle spread an arc of light several feet across the floor.

Buzzt, buzzt, buzzt, buzzzzzt.

The sound was coming from above. He held the candle over his head and walked slowly around his room, looking for the creature who was so noisy at this hour of the night. After a minute, he saw it—a fly, in the corner, caught in a spider's web. Struggling against the silky strands of the web, the fly was desperately trying to escape.

Anthony held the candle up a bit higher. In the corner of the web sat a fat spider, calmly watching as the fly tried again and again to escape the web. But each time it flung itself away from the web, it became more hopelessly tangled up.

Anthony was not very fond of flies, but he really didn't like the look of the fat spider. And he couldn't stand to watch the fly suffer.

Buzz…buzz…buzz… The fly sounded weaker now.

Thinking for a minute, Anthony found a pencil on his desk and dragged his desk chair across the room to the corner where the drama was playing out. Holding the candle in one hand and the pencil in the other, he stepped carefully on the chair. On tiptoes, he pushed the pencil toward the cobweb. He couldn't reach high enough. Stepping carefully off the chair, he spotted the trunk he'd packed the day before with his clothes, his toys, and his books.

Dragging the trunk slowly across the floor, Anthony stopped just under the cobweb. He put the candle on the floor and lifted his desk chair to the top of the trunk, testing its sturdiness with both hands. Then, confident that he could make his plan work, he picked up the candle holder and pencil and stepped gingerly onto the trunk, and then onto the chair. The spider, watching Anthony's actions, retreated into a space between the ceiling and the wall. The fly was too busy buzzing and flinging itself around in the web to notice anything.

Anthony poked at the web, but he could only reach the very bottom of it. He stretched himself as tall as he could and held the pencil at the very tip of his fingers. He poked again. This time he caught the web closer to the center, not far from the fly. He tugged on the pencil, and the web pulled away a little bit from the wall. He tugged again, and ripped a hole in the web, right beside the fly.

Buzz, buzz, buzz.

The fly flew away to the far corner of the room.

Gingerly, Anthony climbed off the chair, then off the trunk, put the candle on the floor, lifted the chair, and carried it back to his desk. He put the pencil, sticky from the web, on his ink blotter.

Then, after placing the candle holder on his bedside table and putting out the flame with a short puff, he climbed back in bed and pulled the covers up.

He felt good. Saving the fly from the fat spider was satisfying. For a moment he felt sorry for destroying the spider's hard work, but not for long. He thought again about the helpless fly before he fell back asleep. Looking out for those who couldn't help themselves would be a good kind of job.

Not just saving flies, of course, but all sorts of creatures who needed a helping hand.

The next morning, Anthony's mother woke him early without her usual smile. This morning she wore a sorrowful expression, one he wasn't accustomed to seeing on his normally cheerful mother.

"Hop up, Son. We have to be at the courthouse in just an hour." She smoothed his hair with her cool hand. "I'll ask Emma to make breakfast. You get dressed and meet me in the dining room. Wake up your sisters for me, please."

As he rubbed the sleep from his eyes, Anthony remembered that today was the auction. His mother's beloved townhouse in Georgetown, where he had lived most of his life, was to be sold. Something had happened to the property after his father died, and although he and his mother and siblings had lived there for years after his father's death, now the townhouse and all the furnishings would go to the highest bidder. He didn't really understand why, but after today, the family would live at their grandfather's plantation in the country. His mother had tried to make the move sound exciting, but he knew she would miss the townhouse where she had come as a young bride. Anthony's father had died in 1828, when he was only thirty-three, leaving his young wife to raise five children alone in the house he had left to her.

The following year, in 1829, Anthony's grandfather, John Porter, too, had died, leaving the plantation home and his slaves to Anthony, his brother, and his three sisters. His grandfather had kept a working plantation, growing first indigo, then rice, and he relied on the labor of his slaves to work the crops. Anthony and his family had spent some time at the plantation, but it wasn't home.

As Anthony waited in the dining room for his mother and sisters, he looked around at the familiar items he had used every day that now would belong to someone else. He had never thought about the china with the blue and gold rim or the dining room chairs with the soft cushions, but now he looked at them with new eyes, and he was sad. He would miss this house and all that was familiar in it.

Just then, Anthony heard his sister Eliza. The morning light from the dining room windows facing the river blinded him for a moment as he looked up to greet her. Eliza was simply a silhouette against the light as she walked into the room.

"It's just not fair. Papa meant for us to grow up in this house and for Mama to live in it for the rest of her life. I don't understand what happened." Eliza grumbled, then sighed and kicked at the tuft of the soft oriental rug under her feet. "The plantation is so far away from town. We'll never get to see our friends."

Anthony sighed, too. He had been thinking the same thing. "But at least you've been at school in New Jersey," he said. "I'll be stuck out in the country and haven't been anywhere but here since we moved back from New Haven when I was five."

They heard their mother coming down the stairs towards them. Eliza grabbed Anthony's arm and whispered, "Don't let Mama see you looking so sad. This is hard enough for her without having to worry about us." She bent down to tie her loose shoelace. "We'll be fine in the country. You'll see."

Before he could mumble something in return, their

mother called to them from the hall. "Hurry up, children. We want to be there before the auction starts. Take a look around one last time. Afterwards we'll only have time to pick up the trunks you've packed to take to the country." She put on her hat and held out her hand to usher the children out the door in front of her. Then she turned one last time and stood for a few seconds in the doorway before turning toward the street and joining her family on the sidewalk.

Anthony picked up a small branch that had blown off the oak in front of their house. He dragged it behind him, making a scratchy sound on the pavement. His mother turned to look at him, her eyebrows lifted just a bit, and he picked up the stick and held it off the ground. When she turned her back, he stuck it out in front of him to poke Eliza in the back.

"Owww. Anthony!" Eliza made a face at him as his mother turned once more.

"Not today, Anthony," she said. "I need you on your best behavior." She smiled sweetly at him but held his eyes for a moment and turned back toward the courthouse. Eliza stuck her tongue out at him quickly, with one eye on her mother's back.

As his family walked solemnly to the courthouse, Anthony's mother turned once more. She admonished them to be brave and not show their emotions. She managed another small smile. "It's just a house. It's just stuff that's to be sold today. It won't change our lives one bit in any important way." She stopped to smooth Eliza's hair. Then she turned to face the courthouse steps, held her head up, and led her family through the crowd gathered at the base of the courthouse.

The children followed her up the steps to the landing at the top. The auctioneer had just set up his block and hammered his gavel down on it to begin the sale. The sun glinted off the metal gavel as the auctioneer brought the gavel down a second time.

"What do I get for this lovely town house? And all its furnishings? Well situated in the center of town. Impeccably maintained. Do I hear an offer?" The auctioneer scanned the faces staring up at him for a response. No one spoke.

The auctioneer waited several long seconds. Not a peep came from the neighbors and townspeople who had come to watch the proceedings.

"All the furnishings. The silver, the beds, everything. Let's start it somewhere. Do I hear one thousand?" He swept his eyes across the crowd, looking for a raised hand.

Silence. The auctioneer sighed and waited a moment.

He tried again. "Do I hear one thousand dollars for this beautiful home? It's worth far more."

Again, silence.

Anthony squirmed and stuck his finger inside his collar

to stretch it off his neck. It was getting hot.

Finally, from the back of the crowd a voice called out. "One thousand."

The crowd gasped.

"We have an offer of one thousand dollars. Do I hear another offer? Two thousand?"

Silence.

A gentleman from the back of the crowd pushed his way to the front. As he came through, the crowd moved aside to let him pass, and Anthony recognized his father's former business partner, Mr. Dozier. He didn't look at the Porters standing on the top steps; instead, he stared intently at the auctioneer.

After glancing at Mr. Dozier, the auctioneer scanned the crowd for another response. "Do I hear a second offer? Anything?" The auctioneer wiped a bead of sweat from this forehead. "Well, then, going once." He paused for the count of three and swept his eyes across the crowd again. "Going twice." He paused for longer this time. "Going three times. SOLD, to the gentleman in the brown suit." And he brought his gavel down on the block to end the sale.

Anthony realized he had been holding his breath during the last part of the auction. He let out a long whoosh and looked at his mother, who was looking at her husband's law partner making his way up the steps. She seemed confused, but as she watched him, a smile began to spread across her face. She reached out to grasp the hand of the gentleman who had just purchased her beloved home.

He bowed slightly and took off his hat. "Good morning, Esther. Good morning children. Would you like to stop for a pastry before I walk you back home?" He turned to Anthony's mother and laughed. "If I'd known that none of your neighbors had the heart to turn you out of your home, I would have bid one hundred dollars, not one thousand."

Then turning to Anthony, he said, "Meet me in my law office tomorrow with your mother. I will write up the deed to turn the house and all the property in it over to you when you reach your majority. Now, let's get something to eat before the temperature gets any warmer. It's going to be another Lowcountry Indian Summer scorcher."

As they made their way down the courthouse steps, Anthony thought about the kindness of the gentleman leading them back to the house they thought they were going to lose that morning. He had just rescued them from the spider's web in a way. Anthony resolved again to be that kind of man when he grew up—maybe a lawyer like his father had been? Somebody who saved the widows from losing their homes. Someone who tried to make other peoples' lives a bit better.

Those thoughts receded as they reached the townhouse, and he and his sisters raced inside to unpack their trunks.

Chapter 2

Anthony Toomer Porter was born on January 31, 1828. His father had died eight months before his birth, leaving his wife, Esther Toomer, to raise five children by herself. She was still a young woman when she was widowed. Esther, who had been educated in Elizabeth, New Jersey, moved her family briefly to New Haven, Connecticut when Anthony was a toddler. Although he remembered little about their years in New England after they returned to South Carolina, Anthony's family maintained their connection with their friends in the North.

When Anthony was still a little boy, his mother sent his older brother John to school in Morristown, New Jersey. The other children remained at home to study with Miss Taylor, who came to the house each weekday. Miss Taylor was a strict taskmaster. With her black eyebrows, sharp nose, and eyes like black marbles, she only had to look at one of the children to send flutters of fear up their spines.

Normally playful, the siblings became silent as Miss Taylor entered the children's playroom each morning to begin her lessons.

"Now, Anthony, let's see what you have done with your mathematics. And Eliza, how are you coming with the translation of Virgil? Good. Let me see your heads bent over and the steam coming out your ears so I know you're working hard."

Anthony caught the eye of his older sister Eliza and dared to smile a bit as he saw her mouthing Miss Taylor's final instructions along with her, her head dutifully bent low.

Miss Taylor didn't believe in spoiling children and frowned each day when Esther interrupted the instruction, appearing in the doorway to the playroom to call them all to a midday meal. But she never turned down the food that the cook Emma had prepared, and she sat with Esther at one end of the dining room table while the children ate their meals at the other end.

Often a guest in the house after school hours, Miss Taylor sometimes forgot to turn off her teacher face and turn on her guest face. She'd raise those dark eyebrows as Anthony ran though the hallway past the sitting room or Charlotte giggled with a girlfriend in the entry way.

One evening, when Esther was entertaining several of the neighbors as well as Miss Taylor in the sitting room, the children ran to the playroom with the neighbor children who had come to visit with their parents. Normally on Friday and Saturday nights, the Porter house was filled with the laughter of guests and the rambunctiousness of the children and their friends. Esther didn't believe that children should have to behave like little adults. Although she subscribed to the adage *"Children should be seen, but not heard"* in places such as church, she wanted them to live full and happy lives, so she outfitted their playroom with games, books, toys, and anything else that would provide them entertainment.

On this particular evening, the noise from their play wafted down the stairs and through the hall to the sitting room. Esther smiled at one of the neighbors whose children had come to visit. "Sounds like our children are having some fun tonight. I overheard Anthony telling Eliza that they should act out the play she was working on. Maybe we should have them perform it for us one evening soon."

Miss Taylor raised one eyebrow. "Maybe if she worked on her French as much as she did that silly play, she'd actually accomplish something in the classroom." Silence fell on the room as all eyes turned to Esther.

Esther smiled at the stone face of Miss Taylor. "Maybe so. Maybe she can do both though."

Miss Taylor turned down the corners of her thin lips. "Not likely."

Esther turned back to her other guests and changed the subject.

A few minutes later, loud laughter flowed out of the playroom. Miss Taylor stood up abruptly and left the room. Esther watched her head down the hall toward the stairs. She excused herself and followed.

By the time Esther reached the foot of the stairs, she could hear Miss Taylor in the hallway outside the playroom. "I will not have this sort of commotion. You will behave yourselves like young ladies and gentlemen. DO I MAKE MYSELF CLEAR?"

On those last words, Esther, who had come up behind Miss Taylor in the hallway, stepped in front of her and simply pointed towards the stairs. Miss Taylor looked once more at the children, gave them her best hawk impression, and lifting her head, turned toward the stairs. As they both arrived in the downstairs hall, Miss Taylor turned to go back to the sitting room. Esther cleared her throat and, staring intently at Miss Taylor, pointed toward the front door. For a minute, Miss Taylor looked confused.

Esther continued to point toward the front door. "In the schoolroom, my children are under your direction. In my house they are under mine. Your action is a reflection upon the manners of my children. They are never allowed to disturb my guests, and had it been necessary, I would have anticipated you by stopping their hilarity; but with their innocent enjoyment in my own house, I permit no interference of any kind."

Miss Taylor stood stock still for a moment and then retrieved her bonnet and shawl from the keeping room and left. It was a long time before she ever set foot in the house again — much to Anthony's delight.

Chapter 3

As Anthony's mother looked for someone to take the place of Miss Taylor, they all excitedly anticipated having the family together again for the holidays. Scheduled to return from his school in New Jersey, John was booked on a ship that would sail down the East Coast to Georgetown. Anthony came to breakfast one morning to find his mother in a frantic state in the study. Esther handed their servant Samuel a sealed letter and turned to scribble something on another sheet of stationery. "Samuel, take these to the post office and ask them to send them out as quickly as they can—and the fastest way possible. Here's some money—no worries about the cost." As she handed their servant a second letter, she muttered to herself, "They have to get there. They just have to." She reached for another sheet of stationery and an envelope.

As Samuel left the study, she called out to him. "And as soon as you give them the letters, come back quickly.

I'll have others for you to take." She was writing letters as fast as she could, sending them to everyone she knew in New Jersey.

"Mama, what is going on?" Anthony went over to her writing desk to see what she was busy working on. Reading over her shoulder, he saw *Do not let John take the ship. Send him home over land. No time to explain.*

"Why isn't John going to sail home? I thought he was looking forward to the trip."

"I know it sounds a bit crazy, Son, but I had a dream last night that was so vivid. I saw John on the boat with all the other passengers, and then I saw a huge storm brew up suddenly. The ship broke apart on the rocks. I don't know what happened next, because I woke up with the sound of screaming in my ears."

Anthony put his hand on his mother's shoulder. But he was silent. He didn't know what to say. Her dream frightened him, too.

For the next several weeks, the family waited nervously for any news of John. They didn't hear from any of the friends up north that Esther had written to, but it was unreasonable to expect an answer for several weeks at the least. Assuming that John had not received the instructions to travel home by land, the family was devastated when they heard word of a shipwreck off the coast of North Carolina, in Hatteras. The ship had shattered on the rocks and only one passenger had survived. It was the same ship on which John had been booked.

Quiet descended on the normally busy, noisy house. Not knowing for certain that John was aboard the shipwreck seemed almost worse to Anthony than knowing that he had died. He tiptoed around the house, afraid to break the solemn vigil.

Friends stopped by to distract him and get him to come out to play, but he felt guilty having fun or laughing when everyone was so worried about John, so he sent them away. He tried to read or work on his math, but he couldn't concentrate on anything. Most days he kicked the fallen leaves off the sidewalk as he wandered down to the river to look for any boats coming to the docks, hoping that John would surprise them and be on one of those boats. He sat on the wharf through the afternoon, seagulls flying and squawking around him, and looked toward the ocean, his heart leaping up whenever he saw a boat on the horizon. But John wasn't on any of the boats that docked.

One evening as the family sat down to dinner, the front door opened. They looked up towards the entrance hall, and in walked John. They started screaming as John dropped his bag on the hallway rug. He looked weary from his travels, but totally unaware of the agony his family had been through for the past several weeks.

"John!" Esther cried as she jumped up to embrace her oldest son. "You got the letters in time?"

Anthony and his three sisters shoved their chairs back and raced to throw their arms around John, too.

Laughing, John pulled back from the knot of people pulling him into an embrace. "Yes, I got the letters — three or four of them, by the way. It seems half of New Jersey was instructed to keep me off that ship." He looked closely at his mother. "What was that about?"

"I had a premonition. I know, I know… not the kind of thing to disrupt your plans…. but it was so strong, John, that I had to do something." She held his eye for a long moment. "And your ship foundered off Cape Hatteras and broke apart. Only one survivor."

John whistled low and shook his head. "Wait. You

heard about the shipwreck. Didn't you hear back from any of your friends that I was traveling home by coach and horseback?" As he stared at the serious faces surrounding him all shaking "no," he shook his head as well. "I guess I beat the letters home." He hugged his mother, his sisters, and Anthony closer. "You must have been so worried."

After another minute, John broke away from the family embrace, tousled Anthony's hair, and stepped into the dining room. He pulled up one of the chairs that had been tipped over a few minutes before. "I'm starving. Let's talk some more after dinner. But I will say, there's a lesson in here—that's for sure. Listen to your mother. No matter how strange her requests might be." He paused. "And don't ignore those premonitions or dreams either, I guess."

Chapter 4

Premonitions seemed to run in the family, but not always with a happy outcome. For a time, all of the children were home in South Carolina. John had taken a job in Charleston with a counting house and undertook to manage the plantation, while Anthony and his two youngest sisters studied at home, with the new teacher, W.R.T. Prior. Anthony's oldest sister Charlotte, whose education had ended after the family left New Haven, suffered from terrible headaches. But Charlotte was a great reader, and as Anthony and his other sisters struggled over their schoolwork with Mr. Prior, Charlotte sat in the study reading one book after another from their father's large library, at least on the days when the light didn't hurt her eyes.

One afternoon as the family was vacationing at their summer home on the ocean by Winyah Bay, Charlotte put down the book she was reading, *The Last Days of Pompeii,* and announced, "I am going to be like the blind girl in the book." She sighed and stared out the window toward the ocean. Anthony noticed a single tear run down her face. He went over and grabbed her hand, but Charlotte didn't turn around or say anything. He stood beside her not knowing what else to do.

But Esther did. To distract Charlotte from her gloomy thoughts, Esther called Samuel to bring the carriage around for a ride out on the beach. She shook her head slightly at Anthony and said, "Why don't we go for a ride? It's a lovely afternoon, and we'll probably have a spectacular sunset. We can look for dolphins." Anthony let go of Charlotte's hand as she stood up slowly and nodded to her mother.

Mother and daughter rode in silence with Esther holding Charlotte's hand. Shore birds swooped to the sand and flapped back into the sky, crying out to one another. The waves lapped gently on the shore, but this evening no dolphin fins appeared to break the surface of the water. Charlotte didn't say anything, but after a time, she asked Esther to have the coachman return home since it was growing dark.

"It's still bright, darling. The sun is gleaming off the water. Don't you see it?"

Charlotte looked distraught. "Then I have gone blind. I cannot see a thing. Just grey everywhere."

Charlotte had indeed become like the blind girl in the

last book she read, and a few months later she died.

Anthony was eight when Charlotte died. He said that just before she shut her eyes for the last time, she told him she was going to a beautiful place where there was no pain. Anthony held the memory of those words of his sister all his life, but when he was eight, they brought him little comfort. When he thought of Charlotte, especially in those first years after her death, Anthony felt a pang of guilt that he couldn't do anything to save her. He didn't like feeling powerless.

With Miss Taylor no longer raising terror in the schoolroom, Anthony and his two sisters found their new teacher not much better. W.R.T. Prior wasn't mean, but he was hard, and he didn't have an ounce of humor in him. Anthony and Eliza found that out the hard way. Each morning, Mr. Prior started class long before Anthony was quite awake. Miss Taylor had at least started her instruction after the children had finished their breakfast, often around ten. But Mr. Prior was fond of saying, "The early bird catches the worm," believing that students were at their best early in the morning. And he started class promptly at eight. Even though Anthony's young body servant, Marcus, woke him up in plenty of time to get dressed and down to breakfast, Anthony couldn't get out of bed. He groaned and rolled back over, telling Marcus to let him sleep a few more minutes. He was not a morning person. Neither was Eliza. They struggled to get to the breakfast table by half past seven and then had to gobble their food and rush up to the playroom where Mr. Prior had already arranged the work for the day. Anthony yawned his way through class until lunch. Every time Eliza yawned, Anthony did, too. His yawns triggered hers as well, so during the first few hours each morning, one or the other of them, or both, had their mouths wide open. Sometimes Anthony's yawns were so big, his jaw hurt.

One Saturday afternoon, a time blissfully free of Mr. Prior, Anthony was digging for fishing bait in the back yard and had an idea. Before he walked down to the dock with his fishing pole, he took a jar of dirt and worms to Eliza's room where he found her reading. He held out the jar. Eliza looked up; her eyes lit up as she understood what Anthony had in mind. "Perfect," she said.

The next Monday morning, Anthony and Eliza surprised Emma by being in their chairs before she brought out breakfast. They smiled at each other and bounced in their chairs, eager for once to get to class. Then they raced up the stairs to the playroom before Mr. Prior had even set foot in the house. When he did arrive in the playroom, they were sitting quietly, working on their assignments, peeking up every few seconds to watch him. Mr. Prior smiled, probably thinking he was beginning to make some progress with these two students of his. He stepped over to the small desk he used and started to put his books down. Instead, he jumped back. "What is the meaning of this?" he demanded.

But it seemed pretty obvious to Anthony and Eliza why a dozen earthworms were squirming their way across Mr. Prior's desk blotter.

Mr. Prior introduced Anthony to Latin and gave him long passages to memorize. Although Anthony was a good student and learned quickly, he never understood the Latin he was studying. He spent many a miserable night trying to learn something he didn't understand, and his schoolbook copy of Virgil was spotted with tears from many long hours of frustration. Anthony began to take note of what he liked about his teachers and his education — and what he hated. The second list grew much longer than the first — much, much longer.

On January 31st, 1838, Anthony woke up excited about his tenth birthday. But instead of waiting anxiously to open presents and celebrate with cake, he found himself drawn towards the church where his father was buried. He told Marcus he was running to the church and would be back in a minute if anyone was looking for him. Then he ran out the door and down the street. Climbing over the brick wall of the cemetery, he knelt beside his father's grave. All his young life, he had heard many stories from his neighbors and his family about the father who had died before he was born, and on his tenth birthday, with his hands on his father's tombstone, he asked God to make him a man his father would have been proud of. He asked that his life be spared so he could grow up to be a man and at his death to leave behind as good a name as his father had. Then he ran home before W. R. T. Prior could chide him for being late for his lessons.

Chapter 5

The next summer, when Anthony was eleven, he and several friends went fishing off the coast of Georgetown one beautiful sunny South Carolina morning. The sky, deep blue and clear, and the light breeze from the ocean lulled the boys into a trance as they sat in the sailboat with their fishing poles over the sides. The ocean swells rocked them gently like babies in a bassinet as the sails fluttered overhead. Occasionally one of the boys hooked a fish, and the trance was broken for a few minutes as they all pitched in to haul the fish up over the sides and into the basket in the middle of the boat.

The family servant Samuel, along to keep an eye on the youngsters and to serve them the lunch that Esther had asked the cook Emma to prepare, sat in the bow of the boat, drifting off to sleep and then waking with a start as the boys caught one fish after another or the sails snapped in the breeze. He and the boys felt the sun strong on their skin, cooled by the wind that was picking up from the west. No one noticed the first large cloud appear over the land a quarter mile away. No one noticed the clouds that began to multiply as the sun reached its peak in the sky.

Suddenly, the wind increased and waves began rocking the boat violently from side to side. The boys lurched back and forth across the hull, and the sail swung wildly. Samuel looked in horror as a wave crested over the side. It turned the boat on its side and threw him and the boys almost face-first into the water. As the boat fully righted itself, the tangle of boys tossed in the bottom began to pick themselves up and grab for the sides to hold on. Having gotten his own bearings, Samuel checked to see that the boys were hanging on as the second large wave knocked the boat on its side again, and a third, following close behind, flipped it over. As Samuel was scrambling to find the surface of the water, he felt an arm, grabbed it, and hauled one boy up with him, tossing him over the upturned hull. As he swam around, making sure the others were climbing up on the capsized boat, he saw little Anthony, a few feet from the rest of the boys, go under.

As Anthony came up from being tossed overboard, he gulped for air. Another wave knocked him back underwater, filling his mouth with saltwater. He flailed his arms and legs, looking for air, just as a strong arm grabbed his fingers and pulled him towards the light again. As his head broke the surface, Anthony saw Samuel's face close to his. Samuel threw him over his shoulder and treaded water. Anthony heard one of the boys screaming and then everything became black and silent.

As Anthony came to, he was still over Samuel's shoulder, bouncing along on dry land as Samuel hurried down the street talking soothingly to him. "You gonna be all right, Mr. Anthony. I gots you."

Anthony could see the sidewalk under him and hear Samuel calling for someone to help. In a few more seconds, Anthony was surrounded by arms reaching out, lifting him from Samuel, and wrapping him in a dry blanket. As he heard his mother cry out, he blacked out again.

When Anthony awoke, he was in his room, with Dr. Wragg beside the bed, holding his wrist. "He's going to be fine, Esther. Thank Samuel for rescuing him. I understand the other boys are all home and none the worse for wear. If he hadn't been there and seen Anthony go under, we might have had a very different outcome."

Anthony's mother appeared in his field of vision beside Dr. Wragg. "I'm so grateful to you — and to Samuel. That must have been quite a storm. I think the Howards had their boat nearby and saw it all. They picked up the boys clinging to the hull and pulled Samuel into their boat with Anthony still across his shoulder. They tell me he never let go of him. Just as soon as they got to shore, he jumped overboard and ran all the way to the house with him."

As his mother filled in the gaps of his near drowning, Anthony thought about what Samuel had done. The doctor and his mother continued talking, but their voices drifted into a mumbling in his ears. He pulled back into himself with just one thought—he was lucky to be back in his bed. He thought about the hand reaching down to grab his fingers as he slipped further into the depths of the water. He thought about being tossed over Samuel's shoulder as the black man treaded water waiting for rescue. He thought about Samuel not giving him up, but holding on to him to deliver him safely home to his mother. Then he thought about Samuel—and realized that he had never really thought much about Samuel before. Samuel was just there, in the background, hovering on the edge of his awareness. But now he owed this man his life.

As Anthony fell into a deep sleep, his thoughts crystallized. He would spend the rest of the life he had repaying the debt he owed to this black man.

Chapter 6

A few years later, Anthony's brother John died after contracting a fever. He had been working in Charleston in George Y. Davis's counting house and trying to restore the plantation which had been left in the hands of overseers and agents. Working in the rain for days on end left him with a raging fever, and at the age of twenty, he died, leaving Anthony, his mother, and two sisters. Anthony, still a boy, had lost a father, a sister, and now a brother.

Shortly after his brother's death, Anthony feared he would soon suffer another loss. His mother Esther decided to take Eliza to New Jersey for her schooling, a trip that would take Esther away from Georgetown for several weeks, maybe months. Anthony panicked. He was afraid of losing yet another member of his small family. He remembered the fear he and his family had felt when John was traveling, and he was determined to do anything he could to make his mother and sister safe in their journey. But what?

Anthony thought about how he could control fate. Maybe if he was good and spoke kindly to his sister? Maybe if he cleaned his plate at dinner? Maybe if he worked harder on his Latin and tried not to hate it so much? But although those acts might make his mother (or Mr. Prior) happy, she was going to be gone, not to see his efforts, and he didn't really see how any of that would keep her safe.

One night while saying his prayers, and adding a fervent plea for his mother's and Eliza's safe travels, he came up with a plan. If God listened to prayers, maybe he would be even more interested in the prayers of a young boy who also read the Bible. Anthony scrambled out of bed and lit his candle. A few minutes later, he pulled his Bible from the bookshelf by his desk and opened it to Genesis. Climbing back into bed, he pulled the covers up to his chin against the chill and began reading "In the beginning..."

Every night, Anthony read late into the night. He usually woke up in the morning with the Bible beside him or across his chest, his candle burned to the stub in the holder beside his bed. After painstakingly making his way through the chapters of the Bible for over a month, Anthony had a revelation. His mother still hadn't returned from New Jersey, so he set out to start again with Genesis. When he mentioned his plan at Sunday School, an older friend showed him how to follow along with the Episcopal prayer book lectionary for the readings for each day of the year. The pattern that began with his fear for his mother's safety became a lifelong habit. And after several long months of awaiting his mother's return, and reading the lectionary now every night, his efforts were rewarded when she stepped into the entry hall and called for her two children still at home. Anthony flew down the stairs and wrapped her in a giant bear hug.

Chapter 7

By the time he was fourteen, Anthony was too old for a teacher at home or for the village school, so his mother began looking for a school fit for her only son, but one that would keep him close to her in Georgetown. He had been confirmed the year before. Hearing that Mr. Cotes, an Englishman who ran the most selective school in the Lowcountry, was going to be near Georgetown visiting William Bull Pringle at his plantation, Esther sent Anthony on horseback to meet Mr. Cotes and apply for admission. Anthony's first impression of the one-eyed Mr. Cotes was terrifying.

When he was brought into the plantation to meet Mr. Cotes, the famous schoolmaster looked at him and scowled. Anthony instantly disliked him. Cotes called him closer so he could examine him with his one eye. Anthony could smell the onion on his breath as he stepped closer. He tried to not breathe deeply.

"Scrawny little thing," Mr. Cotes said to Mr. Pringle. "Looks like a strong blast of air would knock him over."

Anthony then endured a long series of questions about his family, after which Mr. Cotes asked him to recite his Latin. Anthony's mind went blank. All those lessons of Mr. Prior's seemed to have disappeared. He stood staring at Mr. Cotes who tapped his foot and said, "Out with it, boy. Surely, you've learned something." Anthony shut his eyes and tried to remember the Latin he had memorized. He managed to come up with a few lines and stumbled through the recitation. He couldn't imagine the afternoon getting any better, and was ready to excuse himself to make the short ride home. But to make matters worse, Mr. Cotes grumbled an offer for admission to the school! And then, as if things couldn't get even more horrible, Anthony discovered that Mr. Cotes' school ran for twelve months with only Christmas and Easter breaks. No more summer fun. Not only that, but he would be studying in Charleston, not Georgetown.

Anthony spent the next year and a half in Charleston, almost a half day's journey from home. Mr. Cotes ran a tight ship with a schedule that made Mr. Prior's eight o'clock classes look like vacation and a schoolwork load that kept the boys busy at their desks all day and into the night. Anthony longed for the ease of a summer day back in Georgetown, with nothing to do but whatever came to mind — sailing, fishing, reading, playing with the neighbor children. He missed Emma's cooking, too. Mr. Cotes sat in the dining room with the boys for every meal, taking account of every piece of chicken, every spoonful of rice, and even every butter bean. Not that he had to worry too much about anything going to waste. The meals were not plentiful, and the boys' stomachs rumbled throughout the classes that filled their days from early morning until evening. Anthony's parcels from Georgetown with homemade baked goods rarely made it from the post office back to the dorm room before he had eaten everything his mother had sent.

Midway through his second year in Charleston, Anthony was stricken with typhoid and seriously ill. Once his mother read the letter describing his illness, she sent Samuel for the old family doctor, Dr. Wragg, who suggested that Anthony come home to his grandfather's plantation, which he was to inherit, and live a carefree life for several months to restore his health. Dr. Wragg prescribed relaxation and sleep — no studies for the time begin. Anthony happily agreed to the plan. From September until May he lived at the plantation, hunting, fishing, and reading whatever he chose. His mother attended to him, and Emma tried her best to fatten him up with all his favorite foods. Not only did he get better, but he also began to change from the scrawny kid that Dr.

Cotes had commented on to a stronger, more fit version of his former self.

By the next September, he was ready to return to school — just not with Mr. Cotes. At Dr. Wragg's suggestion, Anthony enrolled at Mt. Zion College in Winnsboro, a college preparatory school for boys. Taking the river steamer *Anson* from Georgetown to Charleston, he then boarded the train from Charleston to Columbia, for a trip that took eleven hours. From Columbia, Anthony had to take a stagecoach to the college, but it only ran a few days a week. Stopping over for a few days, he reconnected with an old classmate, and although he had been confirmed three years before, he took communion for the first time. The experience transformed him in a way he didn't yet understand. The next morning, Anthony left for Mt. Zion in the coach, and instead of feeling nervous about moving to a town where he knew no one, he was excited. He felt like a new person, excited about his future. He was about to embark on a new chapter in his life, with new friends, in a new school.

About one hundred boys were already on the campus when Anthony arrived. The first thing he noticed was that they looked rough, not like the city boys he had known in Georgetown and Charleston. Rowdy and loud, several of them greeted him as he stepped out of the coach. One tall boy slapped him on the back, almost knocking him over.

Another whistled and nudged the boy next to him with his elbow as he took in Anthony's custom-made suit. But mostly, the others ignored him as they greeted each other on their first day back at school.

As he looked at the crowd milling around the entrance to Mt Zion, Anthony noticed a few other boys dressed as he was. They were definitely in the minority and looked as nervous as he felt. *Don't want my classmates to think that I think I'm better than they are. All that is going to matter here is what kind of student we are, not what kind of family we come from*, he thought.

Anthony looked around the entrance to the campus for a servant he could call over to carry his trunk. Seeing no one like Marcus or Samuel, no one who fit that description, he realized that he was already showing his privilege. He stood a bit taller, grabbed his trunk by the handles and hoisted it up to his right shoulder. He almost collapsed under its weight, but he gritted his teeth and started forward. "Where is the dormitory?" he asked the boy who had slapped him on the back.

"Across the Green. Here, let me help you." The taller boy grabbed one end of the trunk and lifted it off Anthony's shoulder, holding his end and turning to head across the lawn. Anthony walked behind him, holding his end, grateful for the help. *I should remember to thank Mama for teaching us to take care of ourselves some of the time. Most of these boys have probably never had a servant, let alone a body servant.* Anthony looked at the back of the head of the boy carrying the front end of the trunk as if he did things like that every day. *I never really understood Mama's insistence that we learn to take care of ourselves sometimes. It seemed so odd when Mama made me light my own fire and clean my own room when I had Marcus to do that for me every day. But she knew that someday I'd need to do things for myself.* He sighed. *I guess that starts today,* he thought. As they arrived at the door to the dormitory, Anthony thanked the tall boy and asked his name.

"Harrington. John Harrington. Yours?"

When Anthony answered, John said, "Well, Porter, we're roommates. Welcome to Mt. Zion." John stuck out his hand to shake Anthony's. They stood for a minute looking up the long narrow stairs, and then John wiped a trail of sweat from his forehead and bent down to pick up his end of the trunk.

The two hauled the trunk up two flights of stairs and into the fourth room on the left. Anthony looked around in dismay. Dark and dank, the room was tiny, with one bed and a desk on one side, one bed and desk on the other, and a small window between them.

"Not much to look at," Harrington said laughing. "I'll bet it's nothing like your room at home."

Anthony shook his head. "It'll do." After putting his

trunk at the foot of his bed and unpacking his pens and desk blotter, Anthony followed John out of the dormitory and across the lawn to the large dining room. John grabbed a chair at a table near the door and pulled out the one next to him, signaling to Anthony to join him. Anthony looked around him, confused about the dinner. *We are expected to serve ourselves?* But he followed John's lead, and after several servers delivered large, steaming bowls to the center of the table, Anthony plopped some potatoes, what looked like pork chops, and some black-eyed peas on his plate. No one was counting the spoonfuls of potatoes or peas, which Anthony noted gratefully. He didn't miss the meals with Dr. Cotes. And although the food didn't look as appetizing at Emma's, he thought at least there was plenty of it. And it was hot.

After a boisterous meal in the dining room, the faculty introduced the new students to the upperclassmen. After dinner John and Anthony hung out on the Green with some of the new boys in their class. The moon was full, softening the campus and throwing shadows across the buildings. Pointing to Anthony, one of the boys said, "You one of those rice planter folks?" The question wasn't rude, but it wasn't all that friendly either.

Anthony thought for a minute about how to answer. He knew that "rice planter" was another way of saying he was wealthy, and he didn't want to start his first day with his new classmates thinking that they knew all about him before they actually did. He also didn't want to lie. "I was raised by my widowed mother when my father died months before I was born. I'm not a rice planter, but my grandfather was. He died before I was two."

That answer seemed to satisfy the other boys. They smiled sympathetically at him and turned to another boy to interrogate.

Anthony and John made their way back to their room. Classes would begin at 8:00 the next morning, so they thought getting a good night's sleep would be a good idea, but they had no idea what was in store for them when they turned back their covers on their beds.

"Gross! That's disgusting!" Anthony stared as he pulled back the covers to discover hundreds of little critters running across his sheets. "Harrington, look at this!"

But John had made his own discovery. "So. Many. Bugs." He was standing with the corner of the top sheet in one hand staring at the mad dash across the bottom sheet of his bed. Little black bugs scurried in every direction. "What *are* they?"

"No idea." Anthony dropped the sheet and stood for a moment with his mouth open. Then he grabbed the candle he had put on the bedside table and started dipping it toward every bug still visible. *Tssspt. Tssspt.* "Cremation, Harrington."

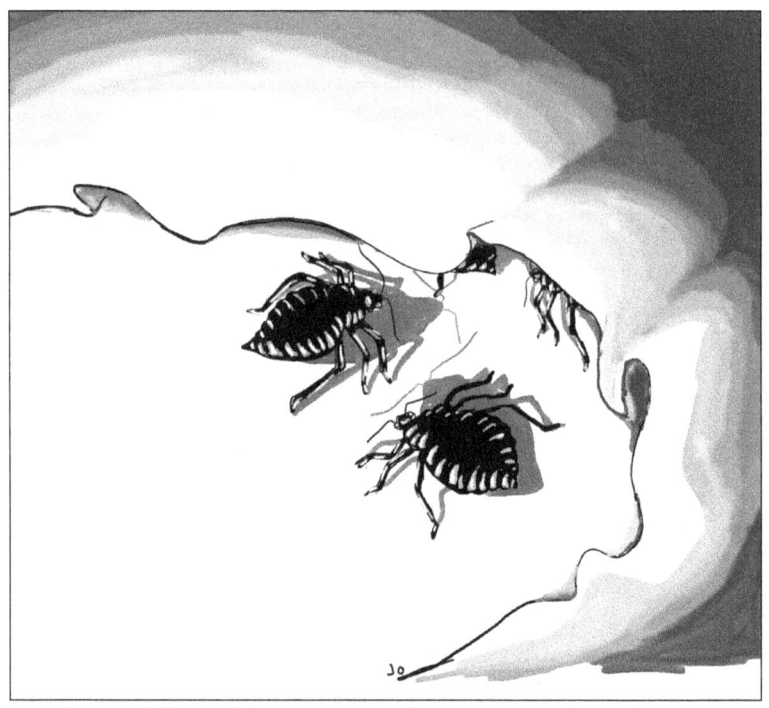

Harrington watched Anthony for a minute and then grabbed his candle. "Let's work on one, then the other mattress. No way I'm sleeping in my bed with all this activity." He moved closer to Anthony's bed. "Here. I'll stand at this end; you at the head of the bed. We'll get them from both sides."

For the next few minutes, the boys zapped the bugs with their candles until they could see no more on the top of the sheet, except little burnt carcasses.

John sighed. "I'm afraid to pick up the mattress, but I'm going to. You burn the ones you see as I hold it up." He grabbed one end of the mattress and lifted it.

"Gross." Anthony grimaced as he saw what was under his mattress. For every bug they had fried on the top of the mattress, they found a battalion below. "We're going to be here all night. Do we have enough candles?"

"I don't care if it takes all night. I'm not sleeping with these little companions tonight. You?"

"No thanks." Anthony swept the candle flame across the base of the bed, cremating dozens of bugs with each pass.

Next, they tackled Harrington's bed, every bit as crawling with bugs as Anthony's had been. It was well after two a.m. when they finally brushed the little crispy carcasses off the sheets onto the floor. They fell into their beds.

What have I gotten into? Anthony had been so busy exterminating bugs that he hadn't had time to think, but now the question was top of mind as he put his head on his pillow, brushing his hand across it first—just in case. "You awake, John?"

He heard a grunt from the other bed. Anthony asked, "Think we'll ever laugh about this?"

"Maybe. Someday. Right now, if I think about it, I feel sick." John lifted his head and held it up with his hand. "But you were pretty amazing with that candle." He chuckled.

"The look on your face when you lifted my mattress. Pretty epic. Like a Trojan seeing the thousand ships of the Greek armada sail up to Troy." Anthony giggled.

John laughed again. Pretty soon they were both laughing hysterically, wiping their eyes and falling back onto the recent battlefield of their sheets. As the giggling slowed down, Anthony wondered what he would write to his mother. She would be waiting to hear about his first day of school. He couldn't tell her about the bugs. But before he had time to figure out what he would write her, he was asleep.

Candles, kerosene, and hot water applied liberally over the next few days finally took care of the bug population that had taken up residence in their room. After eliminating the unwanted guests, the two boys cleaned the room from top to bottom during any free time between classes. Finally satisfied with their efforts, Anthony had a moment to write the letter he had promised his mother.

I arrived at Mt Zion last week, but have been busy getting accustomed to the school and my new routine. In addition to class and studying, we have to fetch our own water, light our own fires, and clean our rooms. I always wondered why you made us children fend for ourselves at times and not rely on our body servants. Now I understand.

Thank you for raising me to be prepared for whatever I encountered. I won't share all of the gruesome details of my first few days, but suffice it to say that my training came in handy. Although I doubt in the way you imagined.

Your loving son, Anthony

Chapter 8

"Oh Romeo, my Romeo," Anthony said loudly, looking up into the rafters of the stage. "Wherefore art thou, Romeo?" He was dressed in a long skirt and a scratchy brown wig, with some red powder on his cheeks. One member of the audience giggled, to Anthony's annoyance. He ignored him and turned to his co-star.

Shortly after beginning classes at Mt. Zion, Anthony and several other boys started a drama club with the support of his beloved teacher Mr. Hutson, in every way the opposite of Mr. Cotes, Mr. Prior, and Miss Taylor. The amateur thespians became so accomplished that they had begun to put on plays for the townspeople, to great applause and enthusiasm. The only issue was that, because Mt. Zion was a prep school for boys, several of the students had to play the female roles, much as Shakespeare's actors had done several centuries before. Anthony, who was tall, but thin, volunteered. Dressed in a wig and long skirt, he portrayed the women characters, and in the comedies, left the audience laughing until they cried. But the more serious plays were another story. Anthony did his best to portray the main female characters, but his voice was changing and sometimes instead of his normal voice, he let out a squawk. When that happened, all he could do was just keep going. For the most part, the audience was kind, and although they may have smiled at his portrayal of Juliet on the balcony whispering to Romeo in the garden below, they rarely laughed out loud.

But if anyone did giggle, Anthony heard it and bristled. *But this is Romeo and Juliet – why couldn't they just suspend their disbelief and go with it? Of course, I'm not a woman, but the actors – and I – are doing the best we can.* As the play progressed, Anthony consoled himself with the thought that no one else had giggled, and the audience applauded each scene with great enthusiasm. *Besides, it was probably Harrington who was giggling. He thinks everything is funny – especially his usually serious roommate playing a woman.*

That first year at Mt. Zion, Anthony had made it known to the other students that he enjoyed a good time, but he was a serious young man. His first test came near Thanksgiving. After classes, he and Harrington were in the sitting room of their dorm hanging out with their other classmates. The boys were discussing how much they would miss being home for the holiday, but since the travel took several days for most of them, by the time they returned home, they would have to turn around and head back to Mt. Zion.

Benjamin spoke up. "I'm sure we won't be getting any turkey for dinner next week." The other boys shook their heads sadly in agreement. "Maybe we could find a turkey or two and sneak them into cook. There's that farmer on the road into Winnsboro who has a whole slew of turkeys. He probably wouldn't miss one or two."

"We can't all go down there. We'd attract too much attention," Robert said as he looked across the room of boys. His eyes stopped on Anthony. "I vote we send our newest classmate. What'da you say?" He looked directly at Anthony and nodded his head.

"Great idea! Anthony! Anthony! Anthony!" The room of boys took up the chant. Anthony noticed even John was joining in.

"Don't look at me. I'd like a real Thanksgiving dinner as much as the rest of you, but I'm not stealing some poor farmer's property. And I hope you won't either." He stared at John who stopped chanting and hung his head a bit.

When the other boys gambled, Anthony did not. And if the boys started to spice their conversation with some swear words, he objected. Surprisingly, rather than pick on him, they respected him and his choices. It didn't hurt that Harrington, almost a foot taller than the other boys, was

Anthony's good friend and roommate. No one wanted to mess with him.

Life at Mt. Zion was difficult, but pleasurable, with time for fun, time for the theater, and time for serious study. Anthony was happy at school, even if it was hard for a pampered boy from Georgetown. But then he met a girl and fell in love for the first time. He thought of nothing but her every minute of every day and counted the hours until he could go into Winnsboro to meet her. School and the acting company took a distant second place to his girlfriend. They walked together often, and he visited her family every chance he had. He was sure she returned his feelings.

One afternoon, after a long walk and conversation, they sat on her porch swing as they had many times before. The night was cool, a late fall evening with an almost full moon just rising over the trees. As they talked, Anthony felt sure that this was the beginning of his future. He hadn't said anything about his feelings before. This time, however, Anthony couldn't hold them in any longer, and they spilled out in one long declaration of his love.

He waited, longer than he had expected, for some reaction from her. To his surprise, his true love sat still for a minute, looking at her hands. She twisted her opal ring and started several times to speak, but never said a word. After a few long agonizing minutes of total silence, she excused herself and went inside, leaving Anthony in the swing feeling foolish — and a little angry. He stumbled down the porch stairs and walked toward school. The bare trees along the street were etched against the moon. The warmth of the day had settled into a soft coolness with a puff of breeze rustling the orange and yellow leaves strewn along the sidewalk. On another night, Anthony would have felt that life couldn't get any better, but this night he was unaware of the beauty around him. He kicked at some piles of leaves and muttered under his breath, not paying any attention to where he was going. His thoughts leaped from disbelief to annoyance to shame, sometimes all three at once.

He stomped up the stairs to his room, not speaking to Harrington who turned to greet him. Yanking his chair out from under his desk, he rummaged around his desk for some stationery and a pen, muttering over and over again under his breath. "I am a fool!"

Harrington, who had lived with Anthony for a year and a half, knew enough to leave him alone. He took his books and his paper and left the room.

Anthony scribbled on the stationery.

Dear Mother,

I have decided that I do not want to go on to college. As the head of the family, I feel it is important to take over the operation of the plantation. A business education would serve me far better for that purpose than college would. I intend to leave prep school, and return home shortly to find occupation in a rice house. Please use your connections to ask if anyone could use my services.

Your loving son,
Anthony

Chapter 9

A month later, Anthony began an internship that lasted for three years at the rice business of Robertson and Blacklock on East Bay Street. He was seventeen, unpaid, and working from early morning to late evening. The small stipend he received from his family was enough to live on if he was very frugal, but he wouldn't receive his inheritance for several years.

Serious about learning all he could of the rice business before he inherited his grandfather's plantation, Anthony made the most of the time at the counting house. With his little time off from work, he taught Sunday school at St. Michaels and enjoyed theater and an occasional dance. Mindful of his role as a Sunday school teacher, he avoided activities that would place him in a bad light with his students or their parents.

One evening, returning from visiting a relative, he encountered a group of five young men on King Street, all children of his family's friends in downtown Charleston. They were headed toward him, laughing loudly and shoving each other as they spotted him.

"Join us, Anthony," one of them encouraged. "We're heading for a night on the town."

When Anthony shook his head and said he was walking home, the others gathered around him, insisting that he join them for their plans. Two boys grabbed his upper arms, lifting him up and turning him back in the direction they were going. They walked along for a minute, jostling each other and cracking jokes. Anthony was caught up in the group, but once he heard their destination was the Bar Room at the Mills House, he tried to make his way out of the crowd.

"Thanks, but I'm on my way home. It's been a long day, and tomorrow will be another long one. You all have fun." He turned to continue his journey down King Street.

"Nothing doing. You're coming with us." One large boy took Anthony's shoulders and yanked him back in the opposite direction. "Time for this boy to lighten up."

"I'm tired. Leave me be, and go on without me." Anthony tried to pull away, but the others protested.

The large boy with his hand on Anthony's shoulders

reached up to rub his hand on Anthony's hair, messing it up. "Just one drink with us. Don't be a stick in the mud." Laughing, the others pushed in toward Anthony and kept him among them, trapped in the center of the pack.

Realizing that he was stuck for the moment, Anthony laughed and went along, all the while plotting his escape. As they approached the Charleston Hotel, he broke away from the grip on his shoulder, pushed through the crowd on the street, and bolted for the front door. When he reached the inside, he turned around to face his captors. The boys caught up with him in the lobby, backing him up and cornering him against the desk.

Anthony was angry. "One step closer, and you'll wish you'd left me alone." He put one fist up and took a small knife from his pocket with his other hand. As he held it up, the laughing stopped, and the boys backed away.

"Sheesh, Anthony. We're just having fun." The boy closest to him shook his head and put his hands up as he carefully took several steps back.

"Yeah, but not my kind of fun — not tonight."

The boys muttered under their breath, but continued backing away. As he saw them turn to leave the hotel lobby, he put the knife back in his pocket and sighed. He spoke to the desk clerk who had watched the last three minutes with his eyes wide. "I'm sorry to have disturbed your evening. I'll leave now. My friends just don't know how to take no for an answer." The clerk shook his head and held his hands up as if to say, "No harm done."

Anthony stepped out into the quickly darkening evening, and turned back toward home. *Stay the course*, he told himself. Distractions, drinking, gambling—all those things his classmates and old friends occupied their free time with—didn't fit how he saw himself, didn't fit his role as the youngest Sunday school teacher at St. Michaels. He remembered his prayer at his father's gravesite on his tenth birthday. *Be a man my father would be proud of.* But it was hard. Sometimes very hard.

Chapter 10

One afternoon, as Anthony settled back in to work after returning from lunch, Mr. Robertson stopped by his desk and requested he go down to the docks to witness a sale of some slaves. "You may know some of them. They are members of two families that Mr. Anderson bought from your mother's inheritance when your father died. As our client, we promised to oversee the sale when Mr. Anderson died. They've been sold to a plantation in Georgia."

Anthony started to protest. "I wasn't even born when my father died. I wouldn't know any of them. Isn't there someone else who can go?" He held his hands up as if to say, "Why me?"

But Mr. Robertson stopped him. "No matter." He tapped him on the back. "You're the only one free at the moment. You'll have to hurry. The boat will be leaving any minute now. We just want to be sure they are on board and on their way. Then we will have discharged our duty to Anderson's estate." Mr. Robertson flung his hands twice in the direction of the door to indicate that Anthony should leave immediately.

Anthony gathered up his jacket and hat and set out for the docks, nervous about having to witness something he dreaded. Since he had gone to Mt. Zion, and then to the counting house, he had not had to come face to face with the reality of slavery. He had grown up knowing the slaves on his grandfather's plantation; he had Marcus, a body servant who took care of his every need as a boy; he knew the house servants in the townhouse in Georgetown, and loved Emma, the cook, who had taken such good care of him—he even had Samuel save his life. Slavery was a way of life in South Carolina. But he despised it. As much as he hated the idea of slavery, he felt there was little a boy or a young man could do to change that.

Anthony hurried down East Bay to the docks. Small clouds scurried across the deep blue of the sky, and the normally calm water of the harbor ruffled with small white caps. When he arrived at the dock, he saw the small gathering of slaves ready to board a ship. One of the older ones spied him on the dock. "There's Mr. Porter's boy! Looks just like his daddy!" He called out, "Mr. Anthony! Save us! Please don't let them take us away from here. Please don't let them break up our families." As soon as the others realized who Anthony was, they, too, began calling to him, pleading for him to intercede in the sale.

Anthony walked up to the old man who had called out to him. "I wish I could do something. I don't have any money, just a small stipend from my family. I don't come into my full inheritance for several more years."

Tears pooled in his eyes as he listened to the two families beg for him to help them. He kept shaking his head, feeling helpless. Walking with them to the end of the dock, he saw them aboard, wishing he could do something, say something to take away their agony.

As the families were herded up the walkway to the ship bound for Georgia, they turned to plead one last time. Anthony shook his head again, tears falling freely on the rough boards at his feet.

A few minutes later, back at his desk, Anthony hung his head in his hands. When Mr. Robertson stopped by for an account of the sale, Anthony kept his head bowed and shook it back and forth. "Please don't ever ask me to do that again. I can't be a party to something like that, even as a witness."

Mr. Robertson put his hand on Anthony's shoulders, but he didn't say anything for a moment. Then he spoke quietly. "I can see that it upset you. I promise to never ask again."

Chapter 11

After three years with Robertson and Blacklock counting house, Anthony was ready to put his business knowledge to the test and take over the plantation left to him by his grandfather. Most of the plantation was in disrepair, having been overseen by agents after John's death, but nothing that some hard work couldn't set right. One of Anthony's first acts as manager was to buy his sisters' slaves. They had been hired out to work for others, so Anthony returned them to the plantation, reuniting families that had been apart for a while. Then he put his mind to improving the land and the slave dwellings on the plantation. Together they rebuilt the fences and the buildings, replacing the old cabins with new ones with brick chimneys. Once the slaves' cabins were rebuilt, he turned to building a small chapel on the plantation. Anthony rose each morning, excited to start the day. As the chapel rose from its foundation, he couldn't wait for it to be finished. Most of the time he supervised from his perch on his horse, but sometimes, he wanted to be more directly involved in bringing the chapel to life, so he climbed up on ladders, working alongside his slaves to nail down the roof. As soon as it was complete, he organized a church service for all on the plantation with one of the enslaved men as the minister.

Then he set his mind to childcare for his workers on the plantation. Often children, even tiny ones, went to the fields with their mothers, or they were kept behind in a cabin with an older woman who could no longer work in the fields. But Anthony wanted something better for the children on his plantation. He had a separate building created for the children to play and be cared for during the day.

Although he continued to keep the slaves he and his sisters had inherited and the plantation benefitted from their labor, he continued to hate the idea of slavery. But under South Carolina law in the early 1800s, a slave owner's hands were tied. For many years, slave owners had been able to free their slaves when they wanted, and many did. But when Anthony inherited his grandfather's slaves, he couldn't free any of them.

One afternoon, while directing the digging of a ditch for a rice field, Anthony watched several strong young men work in the blazing sun. *I wonder why they never rise up against us? Father Hutson says if it weren't for our system, these men would be running wild in Africa. The Methodist minister at Mt. Zion said the same thing. But who are we to decide that they are better off working in South Carolina without any say in how their lives are run? I try to keep them happy – I provide a good home, good food, warm clothing, and religious teaching, and I never ask them to work longer than I would work myself. But the whole thing is just is wrong.* Anthony watched two egrets soar overhead and skid to a landing in the pond across the ditch. *Those birds are as free as I am. These men are not. It isn't right.* He mopped his forehead and moved his horse to the shade. *I think I was born opposed to slavery. I can't remember the time when I did not hate it.* As he called to the men to take a break and get some water, he thought about his options. *I cannot set them free; the law forbids it.*

Anthony knew that in the past, sometimes slaves had been set free by grateful men and women who, often in their wills, requested that one or another of their slaves be emancipated, but South Carolina's laws since the mid-1700s had made it increasingly difficult to free any slaves. The law of 1820 made it impossible for Anthony to give his slaves their freedom without an act of the legislature, which Anthony knew would not happen.

I cannot take them to many Western or Northern states – against the law as well. If I could take them to a free Northern state, what would become of them? I cannot provide them the means to live and feed themselves without the money from the plantation, which requires their help to be profitable. It's a vicious circle. I need their work to turn a profit to provide for my sisters, my mother, for me, and for them, and I need the profit to help them if I send them to a free state to be free. So, if I set them free up North, I cannot provide for them or for my family.

His thoughts were interrupted by a tugging on his sleeve. He jumped down from his horse to hand the men some cool water.

Except for his conflict about slavery, Anthony found life as a planter to be pleasant—he had his horses, his dogs, his books, neighbors and friends who socialized often, church on Sundays. But the occasional matchmaking that his mother and her friends arranged was not to his liking. Ever since he was rejected by his first love in Winnsboro, he wasn't interested in falling in love again. Overall, he had most everything that should have made him happy. But something kept nagging at him.

One evening after a long day of work, he was sitting on the end of his bed, in front of the fire, tired to the bone. As he pulled off his socks, he paused and stared into the fireplace. He was overcome with a feeling that he had missed something—that he had missed what he was supposed to be doing with his life. With one hand on his sock still, he thought about his life on the plantation.

Nothing to complain about. In fact, I have much to be thankful for. But then why do I feel so empty? He finished undressing and climbed into bed. As he stared at the ceiling, he couldn't shake the sense that there was something else he should be doing with his life. But what?

He thought about the prayer he had made on his tenth birthday. He wanted to be a man his father could be proud of. He thought his father would *approve* of him, but would he be *proud* of him?

Anthony remembered the feeling he had the night that he rescued the fly. *Am I doing anything to help others? Yes, I've been taking care of Mother and assuring that the plantation will support my sisters. And I try to make the lives of our enslaved workers as comfortable as I can, short of giving them their freedom.* He wished he could do that for them as well, but he knew that his hands were tied by both the law and practicality. He thought about Mr. Dozier who had purchased their home in Georgetown only to return it to them the same day. He could follow his father and his partner into law and help others that way, but he instinctively knew he wasn't cut out for a law practice.

As he lay awake thinking about the choices he had made, he tried to remember when he was the happiest. Thinking back over his twenty-three years, he realized that he was happiest when he had been teaching Sunday School or setting up the church for the enslaved workers on his land. *Have I missed my calling? Should I become a minister?*

Before the sun rose the next morning, he tapped lightly on the door to his mother's room. She woke up and called to him to come in. As Anthony sat on the edge of his mother's bed, she sat up and took his hands. "What is it? What has happened? Is everyone all right?" Her eyes were wide and full of questions.

"Everyone's fine. I'm sorry if I startled you," Anthony whispered. "I've been up all night thinking about my life, and I've made a decision. I couldn't wait to tell you."

Esther looked both relieved and exasperated. "Well, what is it that couldn't wait until the sun came up?"

"I'm going to study for the ministry."

As she rubbed her eyes, Esther sighed. She started naming all the reasons that he should continue running the plantation.

Anthony shook his head. "I know. I've thought of all of that. But I know this is what I'm meant to do. Just thinking about it makes me happy."

"Well, then, let's talk about it some more in the morning. I, for one, could use a bit more sleep. But if this is what you want, then do it." Esther put her head back on the pillow. "Now get some sleep, Anthony."

That morning, after the sun rose, Anthony rode into Georgetown to speak with his rector. Sitting down with him in the church office, he shared his midnight revelation.

"What took you so long? I've always thought you'd be perfect for the ministry. Let's let Bishop Gadsden know. He'll be able to guide us on your next steps." Reverend Hanckel leaned across his chair and slapped Anthony on the shoulder. "Best news I've heard in a long time."

Chapter 12

Anthony began studying the Greek and Latin he needed to pass the first examinations to become an Episcopal priest, but at the same time, he had to arrange for the care of the plantation. Afraid that whoever purchased it would break up the families who had lived there for several generations, first with his grandfather, then with the overseers, then with John, and now with him, he looked for someone who would promise to keep the enslaved families together. Settling on a good Christian man from Pawley's Island, he then set his attention on learning the horrid Latin that he had hated so much as a boy. This time, however, at twenty-three, he jumped into his studies with excitement.

Traveling back and forth from Georgetown to Charleston, sometimes by boat, for the various stages of his education and examinations, Anthony usually used the eight- or nine-hour boat trip to study. But one morning, as he boarded the ship, he spotted a young woman sitting quietly on one of the benches. Her face was hidden inside her bonnet, but when she lifted her head to look at him, he recognized Susan, a childhood friend who had moved away years before to attend school in Annapolis. He almost didn't recognize her; it had been almost fifteen years since he'd seen her last. Intrigued by her beauty, he moved to take a seat nearby. Although six years had passed since his heart had been broken by the young woman in Winnsboro who had rejected him, for once he was grateful to her. He could feel his heart soar as Susan spoke his name.

"Anthony, is that you? Oh, it's been so many years! What are you doing now? How is your mother?" Susan's eyes sparkled and her mouth curled into a smile as she shielded her eyes from the sun to take a better look at him. "It's so good to see you!"

Miss Susan Atkinson and Anthony were married in December, on the same day as his parents had wed, in the church that he and Susan had attended as children in Georgetown. Shortly after, they were on their way to Charleston for Anthony to become the lay reader of a mission church on Ashley Avenue while he waited to complete his studies.

Calling the Church of the Holy Communion a church was a stretch. For his first sermon, Anthony preached to eight people in a second-floor storeroom of the United

States Arsenal. He looked around the room and wondered what he had gotten into. The walls and floors were bare, and the stairs were more like a large ladder. Wind whistled through the closed windows and up through the opening in the floor. It was freezing in there. It was all Anthony could do to keep his teeth from chattering as he read the gospel. The handful of parishioners huddled in their thin coats and hunched over against the cold. But he noticed that the eight of them listened intently.

Anthony was disappointed by his first service—the room and the number of attendees was not what he had hoped. Nevertheless, after his first sermon, the word spread that a new young priest was serving in the community, and the size of his congregation doubled for the evening service. Over the next weeks and months, the congregation continued to grow from the original eight to many, many more. Enough that he decided to build a real church.

One Sunday, Anthony preached at St. Michaels and asked the members of that wealthy congregation to contribute to building a mission church for the poorer Episcopalians in the northern part of the city. His old employer, Mr. Robertson, scolded him for speaking so directly to the Sunday crowd at St. Michaels, but one old friend stopped him on the street and slapped him on the back. "It was good to see a young man get up in old St. Michaels Church and preach a sermon like that. You did shake up the bones! Why, you made them all look up and wonder!"

Others agreed and were moved by his words. Soon Anthony had enough money to start a new building.

Over the next few years, the congregation of the Church of the Holy Communion continued to grow, and Anthony looked for ways to help the poor in the surrounding neighborhood north of Calhoun and between King Street and the Ashley River. One afternoon as he was walking back from Kinloch and Sons on Prioleau Street, he spotted one of his parishioners. He noticed that she wore the same dress she had on at the Sunday service, but this time he saw that the hem was torn and her sleeves were smudged with dirt. He stopped to speak. "Afternoon, Mrs. Timmons."

She looked up as he stopped in front of her. "Afternoon, Dr. Porter. I was just walking to the market."

"I'll walk with you for a few blocks. It's on my way." He stepped alongside her. "How have you been?"

She sighed and shrugged her shoulders. "Ever since my husband died, I've been finding it difficult to feed the little ones. Walter never made much money, but it was enough for a home and food. We even had some left over for new clothes now and again." She looked down at her tattered hem and dirty gown and pursed her lips. "Not any for that any longer."

Anthony didn't know what to say, but he smiled sympathetically and patted her shoulder. "Things will improve, Mrs. Timmons. Have faith." As they reached his corner, Anthony turned towards home and said goodbye.

Have faith? Things will improve? What nonsense. Why did I say that? How are things going to improve? There aren't any jobs for widows. Even though the church cares for widows and orphans, it cannot alleviate all of the poverty all around this part of Charleston.

Anthony felt terrible. He had been spending so much time trying to build his church, he hadn't paid enough attention to the people in it. He walked the rest of the way home in thought. Mostly he thought about how his mother and his family were almost turned out of their home when he was a boy, and how Mr. Dozier's kindness let them stay in the home they all loved. He knew he had been lucky; he knew so many of the people who lived in Charleston around his church had not been. He thought about his vow on his tenth birthday and about the spider in the web. *Am I doing all I can to help the people who need it?*

As he entered his house, he looked for Susan, hoping to share with her his concerns. After checking the study, he climbed up the steps to the bedroom. There he found her bent over a pillow case, embroidering the edge. As he walked over to sit beside her, he had an idea.

"That's beautiful, Susan. I've never thought much about

the sewing you work on every day, but now I'm curious. How did you learn to sew?"

Susan laughed. "How? I guess my grandmother taught me when I was a little girl. I really can't remember. Seems like I've been doing needlework or sewing all my life." She put down the pillow case and took Anthony's hand. "But why this interest all of a sudden? I've been sewing all our married life." As she looked more closely at him, she said, "And why do you look so upset? What's happened?"

"I've just had my eyes opened. I feel like I haven't been paying attention to what's going on around me." He squeezed Susan's hand.

"What haven't you seen—besides your wife sewing every day, all day?"

Anthony ignored her question. "Do you think you could teach another woman to sew? I mean, to sew practical things? Not decorations on pillowcases, but children's clothing, undergarments, that sort of thing?" He sounded excited.

"Of course. It's not hard, just requires some patience. Why? What are you planning in that mind of yours?"

"I'd like to start a clothing factory and employ the women in the parish. If you can teach them to sew, and I can find a place for them to work, we can help them support themselves." Anthony dropped Susan's hand and jumped up. "I'll go to the bishop and see if he has any ideas about where we can set this up. In the meantime, what if I bring some of the widows in the parish to the house and we can see which ones can already sew and which ones you will need to teach?" Before Susan could answer, he started pacing around the room. "I'll ask Mrs. Timmons for her help identifying who to invite at first." Anthony turned toward the door, ready to put his plan into action. "Then I'll go to Kinloch's and see if they will sell what our ladies will make. We'll have to have a market already set up. I'll ask what type of garment they think they can sell."

Susan laughed and called to him as he headed down the stairs. "I guess I'll gather up my needles and threads. But Anthony, you might think about buying some sewing machines for your new business."

But he was already out the front door, on his way to find Mrs. Timmons at the market and set his plan in motion.

In the next few months, Anthony opened an industrial school near Holy Communion, training young women to sew. First, they made simple items such as underwear, but then they expanded to making all sorts of clothing. Once the Civil War began, they made the uniforms for several regiments.

Busy with his growing church and finding ways to help the poor in his parish, Anthony nevertheless could not help but be aware of the excitement and the discontent in the air in Charleston. Talk of secession was everywhere that Anthony went in the years leading up to the war. Of course, not everyone in Charleston was for seceding from the United States. One friend, James L. Petigru, a well-respected gentleman, thought the idea was crazy. Anthony ran into him one afternoon as Petigru was coming out of his home on Broad Street.

"Dr. Porter! How are you this fine afternoon? We don't usually have such beautiful weather this time of year, certainly not without our famous humidity. I hope you are able to enjoy this glorious day." He stopped at the end of his walkway.

Anthony stopped as well. "On a day such as this, it's hard to think about the heavy topics everyone seems to be discussing these days. James, how do you feel about secession? It's all anyone can talk about—before church, after church, in the streets, even in our friends' homes. I haven't said anything about it from the pulpit, but I know some of my parishioners expect me to."

Petigru shook his head seriously. "I know. I think our neighbors and friends have gone a little crazy. I think we're looking at a war if we secede. Anyone who thinks otherwise is being naïve and foolish. I think we should do everything we can to avoid a war. But my position isn't very popular these days." He smiled. "But we can hope they come to their senses before it comes to something serious."

Anthony shook his head in agreement. He had heard a few days before that Petigru had commented, "South Carolina is too small for a republic but too large for an insane asylum." He agreed.

As the chaplain for the Washington Light Infantry, Anthony waited to see whether South Carolina would secede from the Union. He was present for the vote for the Ordinance of Secession on December 20th, 1860. Although he, like his friend Petigru, had misgivings about the possibility of war, most of the young men at the meeting broke out in celebration and cheering as the vote was announced.

If that was the way his friends and neighbors were going to go, the die had been cast. Anthony put his misgivings aside and supported his home state in its attempt to secede from the Union. As chaplain of the Light Infantry, Anthony preached the first sermon to Confederate troops. He was with the troops on the night of April 11, 1861, when he was awakened by a loud noise in the early hours before dawn.

Grabbing his pants and tugging them on, he stepped outside of his tent as others were doing the same. "What was that?" he asked one of the men gathered beside him.

"Sounds like cannon fire. Over toward the fort." As the men looked across the city toward the noise, they could see the sky light up with each burst of fire.

The Confederate army had fired on Fort Sumter. Major Anderson, the Union officer in charge of the fort, put up

Fort Sumter, April 12, 1861

such a fight that when he finally surrendered, Confederate General Beauregard allowed him to salute the Union flag as it was taken down from the flagpole, and the Confederate soldiers gave him three cheers. But the civility of the first battle of the war was not to continue.

Chapter 13

As the war stretched on, the Washington Light Infantry decided to stay in South Carolina rather than go to Virginia where most of the fighting was taking place. Anthony and his friends promptly formed a new volunteer regiment that would go to battle with Anthony as chaplain. Over the next few years, Anthony tended to the soldiers of first the new regiment and then the 25th South Carolina Regiment. He set up a field hospital near the battlefield in Virginia for the wounded, both Northerners and Southerners. The wounded and dying soldiers were comforted having Anthony nearby. He sat beside their beds, listened to their stories, their fears, and their regrets. He wrote letters to their loved ones for them, and brought them water and whatever little comforts he could find. He never distinguished between the Northern soldiers and the Southern ones. They were all young men in need of his ministry.

Often, when he wasn't in the field hospital, he found himself in the crossfire of the battles. In Virginia, after receiving word that his young brother-in-law had been killed — shot through the forehead in a recent battle — Anthony set out to find the body for burial. Doing so, he then hired a driver to help him transport his brother-in-law's casket home. On the journey, they saw dust up ahead as horsemen rode straight toward them. Anthony knew that they couldn't outdistance the horsemen and worried that they were the enemy. Peering intently at the men bearing down on him, he realized that they were indeed Yankee soldiers. Anthony leaped out of the cart. Conspicuous in his Confederate uniform, and knowing he would end up in a Yankee prisoner-of-war camp if caught, he shouted to the driver, "Keep going. I'll meet up with you in town if I can!" He cut across a field and ran into the woods moments before the Yankee soldiers on horseback stopped the cart.

"After him!" the officer in charge of the Yankee soldiers hollered. The Yankees dug their heels into their horses' flanks and sent the dirt flying as they rode straight for the woods. Anthony ran deeper into the woods as he realized they were pursuing him. Staying just ahead of the soldiers, Anthony zigzagged through the trees, hiding in ditches and behind fallen logs just moments before the Yankees rode past. The chase went on for fifteen minutes with Anthony doubling back time and again to elude capture. As he hid

behind a tree to catch his breath, he watched the lead horse get closer by the second. All at once, the soldiers pulled up on their reins and turned back to the road. *Probably worried they'd get lost in the woods. One Confederate soldier wasn't worth all the trouble,* he thought as he slowly made his way back to the road to walk the rest of the way to town.

In June of 1862, back in Charleston, Anthony ended up in the middle of the battle by Secessionville, with bullets whizzing past his ears. Unconcerned about his safety, he helped soldiers bring bodies and wounded soldiers, one after the other, from the battlefield to the rear where the doctor was taking care of those who had a chance of surviving their wounds. In the span of a few hours, he helped carry the bodies of four of his friends to the rear of the battle—four friends he had been with the night before, singing in his tent. Returning to the fighting, he saw one young friend running towards him holding up his bloody hand. "The Yankees have blown off my thumb!" he shouted as he ran, blood streaming down his arm, toward Anthony.

"You'll be fine. Keep heading straight past that large oak. The doctor is just past there in the medical tent." Anthony pointed the way and then turned back to the battle. Moments later Colonel Hagood rode out of the woods and asked Anthony what on earth a chaplain was doing in the middle of a fierce battle.

"Waiting to see what I can do," Anthony said as another bullet flew past them both and thwacked into a tree.

"Well, then I order you to leave."

Anthony looked at him and shook his head. "You are not my colonel, and I refuse."

They both laughed. As the next round of bullets whizzed by, Hagood said, "Well, then, go behind that stump over there and stay there, or you will certainly be killed."

"I'll obey that order!" Anthony ran and dove behind the stump just as two bullets ripped into it. Still in range of the guns, he decided the stump wasn't actually the best protection, so he threw himself back into the battle to help bring the wounded out.

During lulls in the battles, Anthony went back into town from his regiment's encampment on James Island to check on his family, preach at the church, and visit the wounded in the hospitals. Since the start of the war, Yankees had been shelling downtown Charleston from their position at Fort Johnson. Many of the old homes had been rendered unlivable and the families displaced. Several old friends, including Dr. Wragg from Broad Street, Allston Pringle from lower King, and A.O. Andrews from Hazel Street, had moved into the Porter house on Rutledge. The house wasn't huge, but with twelve rooms, they found a place for everyone who needed a roof over his head.

Anthony continued to go between the regiment and his family and church. By late 1864, the tide of the war was turning in favor of the Yankees. When General Sherman was marching through the South on his famous March to the Sea, burning cities in his path, the Confederates moved the Yankee prisoners from the prison camp at Anderson to Florence. The train cars carrying them frequently stopped on the tracks near the Porter house on Rutledge, and knowing that the prisoners were often starved and mistreated, Anthony sent his two young boys to bring the Yankee prisoners some food. After one such excursion, his oldest son came running home calling for his father.

"Papa, Thomas and I—we saw him die. We saw one of the prisoners die." Anthony's oldest son Toomer threw himself into his father's arms, sobbing. "All the men looked so sick. They could barely reach out for the food we brought them. One said 'thank you,' but the others just stared at us. Their hands and their arms were so bony." He looked up into his father's face. "And then one groaned and slumped over. The guard pushed us away, but we knew. We knew that man had died." He put his face back into Anthony's shoulder and sobbed again. Thomas, the younger boy, just stood by and watched his older brother cry. Anthony reached over and pulled him into an embrace as well. As he hugged his two boys, he thought about his conversation with Mr. Petigru before the war. He wondered if those young men who had cheered at the news of secession and at the firing on Ft. Sumter regretted their enthusiasm for the war. He imagined that they did. He whispered to each of his young boys, still holding tightly to him, "I love you. More than you can know."

Days later, Toomer was stricken with yellow fever, a disease that could be fatal, although must people survived after three or four days of illness. Shortly after Toomer showed the first signs of chills and fever, Thomas and other members of the household came down with yellow fever as well. The others recovered quickly, but Toomer, his first-born son, died after a violent illness.

In the midst of war, Anthony and his wife Susan had little time to grieve. The very evening that little Toomer died, another child in the neighborhood died of yellow fever as well. Anthony had to go comfort the parents when he needed comfort himself. After Toomer's death, he threw himself into his role as chaplain to the infantry, crisscrossing the states from South Carolina to Virginia.

After years of the Union forces shelling the city and the fire of 1861 which had destroyed many of the old homes, Charleston residents who could leave, had done so. Anthony, Susan, their children, his adopted daughter, their servants, and several friends escaped to Columbia to stay in the capital city, living with his family friend, Dr. Reynolds, and his family near the center of town. By late 1864, General Sherman had burned his way through the South and was heading toward South Carolina. The Confederate troops, spread thin between trying to defend Augusta and Columbia, evacuated Columbia, leaving behind a few soldiers and many women and children. Major Green ordered the cotton stores, one of the South's most valuable commodities, brought into the streets and burned, rather than let the Union troops get their hands on it. Worried that burning the cotton could be a dangerous move for those remaining in the city, General Wade Hampton ordered the soldiers to not burn the cotton stores, but his orders did not reach all the remaining troops. As retreating Confederate soldiers began to riot and loot in the town, martial law was declared on February 16th,

1865. Anthony and Dr. Reynolds anxiously watched the escalation of tension and violence in the city, but they had little hope of escape. The rail cars leaving Columbia were loaded with Confederate weaponry or employees of the Confederate government, leaving no room for civilians, and with such chaos all around them, they didn't know how to get their families out of the danger.

As the first of Sherman's troops began to arrive in Columbia, some of Anthony's neighbors thought they could win the protection of the Yankees by offering them the stores of alcohol left behind. It wasn't a good idea. The Yankee soldiers, who hadn't eaten or slept in twenty-four hours, quickly became intoxicated. Chaos was everywhere. As quickly as one fire was extinguished, another was set. All of the houses on Dr. Reynolds's street, except for his, were burned. Matters grew even worse on the night of the 17th, when high winds made it difficult to contain the fires.

Susan peered out of the curtains covering the parlor windows at the Reynolds' house. The night sky glowed with the fires, and embers, like bright fireflies, fell through the trees. Frightened for their lives, Susan begged her husband to do something. She whispered, hoping to not wake the sleeping children. "If we sit here, we're either going to be caught in a fire or be at the mercy of drunken soldiers. We have no real choice. We can throw ourselves at the mercy of General Sherman. If we go to his headquarters, surely he will take us in to protect the children and the women."

Anthony ran his fingers through his hair. He knew he had to do something, but what? It was late, after ten, but the sky was glowing. With martial law, it was against the law to be in the streets, but with so many defying the order, he couldn't imagine a group of women and children would be apprehended. He knew they were in danger if they stayed where they were, but he had no idea what they'd find if they ventured out into the city. There was no good choice, but he knew sometimes it was better to do something than to sit still and do nothing. He knelt down to pick up his sleeping son. "Gather everything we need and can carry and wake the older children. We should leave soon if we're going to go." Susan started immediately to wake the other children.

With only a few clothes and blankets for the children, Anthony, his wife, and their children made their way through the burning, the rioting, and the drunken brawling in Columbia with their household servants and Dr. Reynolds and his family. About a block from Sherman's headquarters, they stopped at Mr. Miot's house, where two federal officers were stationed, and were welcomed inside. Anthony and one of the women stood guard at the entrances.

Fires raged around them, and the drunken shouting in the streets continued for the next hour. Susan and the others huddled in the front room afraid to look out the windows, but they could see the glow in the sky and hear the crash of buildings as they fell to the flames.

Shortly before midnight, Dr. Reynolds stood up and headed out the door to where Anthony was standing watch at the end of the porch. He spoke firmly. "I can't stand this any longer. I'm going home. I've lived in that house almost my entire life and I'm going to protect it or die trying." Dr Reynolds moved to walk past Anthony.

"Don't go." Anthony grasped Dr. Reynolds' sleeve. "You have no idea if it's still standing, and just getting through the streets is dangerous enough. As the night goes on, the destruction increases."

The doctor shook his head. "I can't sit here and wonder what's happening back there. Keep an eye on my wife and daughter. And pray for me." As Dr. Reynolds pushed past Anthony, one of the federal officers staying at Mr. Miot's, a young Yankee lieutenant, stepped out of the shadows. He had been walking around the house, keeping an eye out for looters and arsonists.

He approached Anthony and Dr. Reynolds. "I agree with the chaplain, but as you seem unconvinced, I'll go with you to see that no harm comes to you. Our troops are out of control. No telling what you'll encounter. But maybe they'll listen to me—one of their own officers. I hope, anyway." He stepped in beside the doctor as they turned back toward the fires.

The next three hours were agony for the Reynolds and for the Porters. They sat in the parlor staring at the door and listening for footsteps on the walkway. About three in the morning, they heard footfalls and Anthony jumped up to see who was coming to the door. The Yankee officer opened the door and met Anthony.

"I've come with a message from Dr. Reynolds. All is well at his house. It is still standing, and he thinks it will be safer if the women were there. I've come to escort you back." He looked exhausted, but took a deep breath and the water Mrs. Porter offered him. "The sooner we go, the better. The streets are a little quieter now than when you came here earlier last evening."

Anthony was silent as he stared at the man, several years younger than himself. *This was an officer of the enemy, offering to take them to greater safety. It could be a trick, but what would the Yankees serve to gain from capturing a chaplain and a bunch of women and children? To rob them? Surely the Yankees knew they hadn't been able to bring much of anything with them. But why hadn't the doctor written a note, something to authenticate his request?* The questions troubled him, despite the young lieutenant's seemingly honest character. Anthony made a decision. "I'll go ahead and ascertain the situation for myself. Then, I'll come back and we can walk back to the Reynolds together."

He stepped out into the street and turned toward the Reynolds' house. All of Columbia in that direction seemed to be aglow. As he stood in the middle of the street and gazed in amazement at the destruction, General Sherman rode up beside him. "It's terrible," the general said.

Anthony recognized the general. Desperate and angry, he replied, "Yes, when you remember that women and children are your victims." He had lost all fear, even in the presence of the infamous Yankee, General Sherman.

"It's your governor's fault," Sherman announced.

"How so?"

"Who leaves such a quantity of liquor behind for the invading army? It's not our fault that our men found such large stores of alcohol." General Sherman shook his head with disgust. Before Anthony could respond, a Yankee officer rode up. General Sherman snapped at him. "Andrews, get this under control. I hold you personally responsible. Call up the Second Division and have them put a stop to this destruction. Immediately."

Anthony, relieved that the order to end the rioting had been given, left General Sherman and went on to find the Reynolds house, but with so many houses burned to the ground, nothing looked the same. He couldn't get his bearings. Encountering one drunken group of soldiers after another, he weaved through the city, finding himself back at the Miot house.

When he arrived, he was met at the gate by the young Yankee lieutenant. "Where have you been? I've taken your family and the others back to the house. Everyone is fine — just a few minor burns from some falling embers. But there is despair over your disappearance. Where were you?"

"Where is my family? You've taken them where? On whose authority?" All sorts of wild thoughts raced through Anthony's head, but he demanded that the officer take him to his wife and children. They set out across the city again, but this time the officer led him straight to Dr. Reynolds's home, one of only two structures that hadn't been burned in a ten-block radius. Once settled safely inside and able to determine that everyone was well, Anthony shook the Yankee's hand and thanked him for protecting them through the night.

"I was happy to do it, Sir. Not all of the soldiers in the Union army are like the ones you saw tonight. Some of us are honest, good Christian souls." He introduced himself as John A. McQueen of Company F, 15th Illinois Cavalry.

Reunited with his wife, children and friends, Anthony helped them find beds and blankets and settle down. He then went to find Reynolds who was in the dining room, trying to put the room back in some order. Pieces of china, crystal, and silver were strewn all around the room and piled on the table. Chairs had been upturned; even the curtains had been pulled down. As he reached down to pick up a silver fork under the table, Anthony asked Dr. Reynolds about McQueen.

Dr. Reynolds put a crystal wine glass in the almost empty credenza and took the fork Anthony handed to him. "When he escorted me to my home through the smoldering ashes of the houses in my neighborhood, we found my house still standing, but full of soldiers, breaking into everything and hauling out anything they could carry." Dr. Reynolds shook his head as he placed the fork in an open drawer of the sideboard.

"McQueen entered and ordered the men to drop what they had and exit the house immediately. I guess because he was an officer, they complied. I held my breath waiting for one of them to challenge him, but they didn't. As they left the house, several dropped what they were carrying out, but I could tell that most of my valuables had already been hauled off." Dr. Reynolds paused and looked at Anthony ruefully. "But if it hadn't been for McQueen, I might have lost everything, including my house. Once he was certain the house was secure, he asked if I was comfortable with him returning to the Miot house to bring our wives and children and our servants, back. When I nodded 'yes,' he went among the remaining soldiers in the street out front, and finding several sober ones, stationed them as guards at each entrance and on the roof. Before he left, he organized a fire bucket brigade to toss water on the roof as protection from the fires still smoldering all around." Dr. Reynolds picked up a spoon from under the window.

Anthony listened in awe. This man who had done so much for them was an officer in their enemy's army. It gave him a shred of hope to know that some men on both sides of the battlefields had retained their sense of civility in spite of the horror of the war.

Dr. Reynolds went on. "The children and our wives all attest to his gentleness and kindness. Your daughter's nanny sobbed with relief as they set foot in the house, and grabbed McQueen's hand to thank him."

As Dr. Reynolds spoke so glowingly of Lt. McQueen, Anthony thought of how fortunate they had been in their particular enemy. He left the doctor and joined his wife and children in the parlor where they were fast asleep on the makeshift beds. As he settled down on the parlor rug, he noticed that the edges of the windows around the parlor curtains glowed with the soft light from the dawn and not from the lurid flames of the fires. He said a short prayer, grateful that Sherman had ordered his men to stop the destruction of Columbia. Before he fell asleep, he hoped he would have some way to thank this young Yankee who had shown them all such kindness. At that moment, just before he fell asleep, he had no idea how soon that opportunity would present itself.

Chapter 14

The next morning, Lt. McQueen spoke to Anthony and Dr. Reynolds before leaving to rejoin his regiment. "If you all feel secure here, I will head out to catch up to the Union army as they leave Columbia."

Anthony's first thought was for the safety of their rescuer. "Won't you likely encounter Confederate troops stationed just outside the city?"

"It's possible, but if I don't leave soon, I'll be certain to be separated from the regiment." McQueen put his hand on Anthony's shoulder. "But if you need me to stay any longer, I'm happy to do so."

Both the doctor and Anthony spoke at once. "No, go. We'll be fine here."

Lt. McQueen nodded and turned to the entrance hall.

Anthony called to him. "Wait! Let me write a note explaining why you're not with your regiment and what you did to help us. Many of the soldiers know who I am, so they might be more lenient if you have something from me." He turned to the parlor to find a pen and some paper in the desk.

"I'll get something for you from my office," Dr. Reynolds said. "I'll just be a minute."

McQueen and Anthony stood together in the hallway. Anthony spoke first. "I don't know how I can ever repay you for your protection last night. I doubt we will ever see one another again, but go with the knowledge that you have made a friend of a Southerner." McQueen grabbed Anthony's hand. "And you have made a friend of this Northerner," he said. "Once this dreadful war ends, I hope you will write to me and let me know how you and your family are faring."

Dr. Reynolds reappeared with pen and paper in hand. Anthony hastily wrote a note describing McQueen's kindnesses and requesting his safe passage should he fall into Confederate territory. Handing Lt. McQueen the note, Anthony shook his hand once more. "God speed."

Dr. Reynolds added, "Safe travels, my friend."

Once McQueen was out of sight, heading down the street leading away from Columbia, Anthony and the others set about securing their protection without the aid of the Yankee officer. Sherman had given the townspeople some old muskets for their defense, but they quickly learned that they were worthless. They found a few guns that had been hidden away, and with those they set up a militia to protect themselves. After a month, they were able to move to safer lodgings, and headed north to Newberry. From there they took the train to Anderson.

In Anderson, Anthony met Wyatt Aiken, the brother of Hugh, one of Anthony's classmates at Mt. Zion. Hugh had been killed a few days before in a battle nearby, his brother explained, and Wyatt was on his way to retrieve his body.

As Anthony shook his head with sympathy, Wyatt added that two Yankees had also been killed in the same battle and two wounded. "One of the wounded would have been killed by the soldiers, but he pulled a letter out of his coat pocket—from you!—or so he said." He looked intently at Porter. "Do you know anything about a Yankee lieutenant? McQueen, I think they said, Lieutenant John McQueen?"

Anthony's mouth dropped. "I do! He was the one who saved my family from the crowds of Sherman's soldiers rioting in Columbia. I gave him that letter, but I had little thought that it actually might be useful!"

"One of the soldiers knew of you from Charleston, and he saved McQueen's life—at least until they could determine if the letter was really from you." Wyatt watched the conflicting emotions play across Anthony's face—relief, fear, disbelief. "I'm not sure where they took him after that, and I don't know if the letter was going to save him or not. Our soldiers are pretty riled up about the destruction Sherman's armies have caused in Georgia and South Carolina. They aren't showing much leniency to Union soldiers right now."

"I'll need to find McQueen and explain to his captors that the letter is authentic. Which direction do you think they've gone with him?"

"It's been several days. But the soldier that stopped the others from hanging him on the spot said, 'You must be an uncommon Yank to have a letter from Reverend Porter.' He seemed to want to try to honor your request in the letter. My guess is that they've taken him back to a hospital with all the wounded Confederate soldiers, maybe near Camden?"

Anthony groaned. "We've just come from Columbia, but I must go back. Thank you for this news—and the hope that he might still be alive." He paused. "I am sorry to hear about Hugh. He was a good man, and a good friend. We played opposite each other in several plays at Mt. Zion. He could bring down the house—a scholar and an entertainer." He put his hand on Wyatt's shoulder. "I will pray for him and your family—and that we see the end of this war soon."

After hearing that McQueen might still be alive, Anthony made sure his family was settled comfortably in Anderson and then set out back toward Columbia as soon as he could. He took the train as far as Newberry. From there the tracks had been destroyed by the Yankees, so, disembarking, and unable to find any sort of wagon, horse, or carriage, he started walking. The trip to Columbia took two days on foot, through non-stop torrential rain. When he arrived in Columbia, soaked through and tired, he built a fire in an abandoned barn to dry his clothes, and then set out for Camden, with really no idea where to look for McQueen.

On a hunch, Anthony started with the old Lord Cornwallis house, which was being used as a Confederate hospital. He walked down the halls of the old house, opening one door after another, not sure what he would find. In one room, he spotted a sea of men in tattered Confederate uniforms lying on beds and the floor. Across

the room, in one corner, he spied a blue uniform. He stepped gingerly through the throng of soldiers on the beds and pallets and peered closely at the one soldier in the Yankee uniform curled up on his side on the floor.

"Ahhhhm." Anthony bent down to see the soldier's face just as the Yankee looked up.

The soldier started up off his pallet, and winced.

"Here. Let me help you." Anthony reached down and grabbed McQueen by the wrist as McQueen grabbed Anthony's wrist. Anthony pulled his friend up to standing.

Once on his feet, McQueen threw his arms around Anthony, and said, "Thank God, home again." Then he began to sob.

Anthony wrapped his arms around John, and sighed with relief. McQueen was in obvious pain, but at least he was alive. Now to get him back to his regiment and out of danger.

All eyes in the room were on the spectacle in the corner. One Confederate soldier nudged his neighbor. "Well, that's a sight I haven't seen in this long war. And I've seen a lot of sights."

"Explains a lot, too. Figured that Yank must either have friends in high places or he wouldn't have been in here with us." He called across the room. "What's the story, Yank?"

Anthony turned around to see the audience of soldiers watching the reunion in the corner. "I can tell you that," he said. "This man risked his life to save mine, my family's, and several other families in Columbia just last month. When Sherman's troops were running amuck and burning homes in Columbia, and the Yankee soldiers were drunk in the streets, Lieutenant McQueen led us to safety, secured our safe harbor, and stayed after his regiment left the town to insure our protection. I didn't at first, but I grew to realize I couldn't have trusted him more if he'd been my brother."

One of the soldiers close by stood and shuffled over to grab John's hand and shake it. Others leaned up on their elbows and clapped or whistled. Anthony sat down beside his friend and said, "If you think you can travel, let's figure out how to get you back to your troops."

Over the next week, Anthony, having obtained permission to escort Lt. McQueen to where the federal troops were stationed, found an old buggy and mule and a set of civilian clothes for his friend to wear on the journey. They agreed that John should avoid talking because his Ohio accent would give him away to any curious Southerners.

The mule was so old that he struggled to pull the buggy with both men on it, so Anthony walked the sixty-four miles to Chester alongside the mule. Once there, they took a train to Raleigh and then to Greensboro, and back to Raleigh again, looking for the Confederate general who could release McQueen and give him a safe pass back to the Union side. Finally, after a long journey, they found General Johnston who, after hearing of McQueen's service to the Porters and Reynolds, gave him a pass to return to Union troops without the requisite exchange with a Confederate officer.

The two men parted, exhausted, and overcome with emotion, Anthony to return to his family in Anderson and John to make it back behind the Union lines. As Anthony left, he thought, *This friendship bodes well for whatever happens at the end of this war. It has to end sometime. And whatever the outcome, the North and the South will have to figure out a way to get along. It's not going to be easy, but knowing that there are men like John in the North will make it easier. At least I hope it will.*

Chapter 15

Instead of immediately going back to Anderson, Anthony stayed with General Johnston who asked him to do whatever he could to help the Confederate troops. One evening, several weeks after seeing McQueen safely back to Union troops, Anthony was dining with generals Johnston and Hardee. A soldier interrupted the meal to bring the generals a telegram. Johnston read it, stood up, handed it to Hardee and left the room.

Hardee followed General Johnston out of the room and returned alone. He handed the telegram to Anthony and sat down, putting his head in his hands. "We three are the only ones who know the content of this message," he said quietly.

Anthony opened the folded sheet of paper and read:

April 1865

I have not heard from General Lee for three days, but from the reports from stragglers, he has met with a great disaster. Come to me.

Jefferson Davis

So, this was it. The war was over—or almost over. "Where is General Johnston?" Anthony asked.

"On the train to meet with Davis. He left immediately. If what Davis has heard is true, we will need to begin dismantling the armies. But let's wait to have something confirmed. Keep this to yourself for now." Hardee stood up and reached for the telegram that Anthony held. He spoke quietly, his voice shaking. "It was a gallant effort. But too many lives lost and too much destroyed. We will have a time rebuilding the South." He straightened his stooped shoulders as he folded the telegram and put it in his jacket pocket.

Anthony shook his head solemnly. There wasn't anything to say.

"A disbanding army is a dangerous thing," General Hardee warned, "but let's not get ahead of ourselves. We'll wait to hear something from Johnston or Davis. Let's get some sleep tonight."

For the next two days, the general and Anthony headed west. When they reached Chapel Hill, they received the word they had anticipated—General Robert E. Lee had surrendered. The war was over.

When they heard the confirmation, General Hardee turned to Anthony. "I'll find you a mule to carry you back to your family. They'll need your protection. There's nothing more you can do here, and to stay is not wise. Besides, we'll need people to spread the word of the surrender and let everyone know that the army will be disbanded. Soldiers will be heading home soon."

As Anthony protested, the general spoke firmly. "Go to your family. Return with them to Charleston. There will be much you can do to help rebuild that city, much you can do to bolster the people who will be in despair. You are needed there." He took Anthony's hand in his. "I wish the outcome had been different, but we must accept the reality and look forward." He then called to an orderly. "Find a mule for the reverend, a good one, but not so good that the soldiers might want to relieve him of it in their haste to get home."

Then he turned back to Anthony. "God speed, Porter."

Chapter 16

Leaving his family in Newberry until he could determine what condition Charleston was in, Anthony slowly made his way back to Charleston following much the same path as the one torched and charred by Sherman's army. On his return, he stopped in Orangeburg and presented himself to the Federal officials there to sign the oath of allegiance to the United States government. When he finally arrived in downtown Charleston and walked up the street to his home, he discovered it had been occupied by the Freedman Bureau and all his furniture removed. With no place to live and no money, he was at a loss. But not for long.

Calling on his education in business with Robertson and Blacklock, he went to the business district, and finding a freedman butcher, George Shrewsbury, he borrowed money to purchase goods that were badly needed in the Upstate. Shrewsbury loaned it happily. Then he visited the owners of Kerrisons and several dry goods stores, explaining that he wanted credit to buy food, candles, clothing and other goods to take to Anderson where no stores had been reopened to sell the necessities unavailable in that area. The first trip was so successful that he went several more times between Charleston and Anderson, making enough money to not only pay off his initial debt to Shrewsbury, the Kerrisons, and others, but also to have enough to support his family and their servants.

Back in Charleston, Anthony realized he was the only Episcopal preacher who had returned to the city. He resumed preaching at the Church of the Holy Communion, but what he had to say in his sermons was not well received by all of his parishioners. In his first sermon, he advised his listeners to look forward, not back, and to rebuild their lives with what they had left.

He went on to describe his intent to build a school for the children of the newly freed slaves and to look at the Northerners not as the enemy. At the end of the service, Anthony stood at the entrance to the church to greet his parishioners as they left. Several turned away from him, frowning, and walked around the line of people waiting to speak, but others shook his hand warmly as they headed out the door.

"You've turned into an Abolitionist! What was that all about?" Anthony turned to see one of his cousins scowling at him and shaking his head in anger. He grabbed Anthony's upper arm and shook him a little. "You've gone over to the enemy!"

"Not by a long shot. I feel as you do about the ruin of the South. But abolitionist? What is there to abolish? The slaves have been freed. It's a fact. And I for one thank God for that!" He stopped to smile at a young family leaving the church before turning back to the conversation. "And Cousins Laurens, better to provide an education for them and embrace the change than fight it. We've done that. The war is over. Let us make the best of it and move forward."

Several federal officers walked by, nodded, and smiled as they left. One shook Anthony's hand, simply saying, "Thank you."

Later, as Anthony changed out of his vestments in the back of the church, Governor Aiken found him. "If this is the way our public men shall speak, there's hope for the old land yet; we shall live and not die." He patted Anthony on his shoulder. "Keep it up, young man."

Shortly after, Anthony received a letter from his friend McQueen, notifying him that if he had any trouble with his property, he should apply to General Howard to have it released from the Freedman Bureau. Anthony contacted General Howard who, in turn, requested that General Saxton return the Porter home to Anthony's ownership, which happened promptly. Now that he had money to support them and a home for them to live in, he returned to Newberry in November of 1865 and brought his wife, his two sons, aged three and ten, his adopted daughter, and their servants, home.

Throughout the last few years of the war and the first years following Lee's surrender, Anthony was so busy that he had had little time to dwell on the loss of his oldest son. At his bishop's request, he ventured north to ask for money to build a school for the children of the freed slaves. He left Charleston on April 4th, 1866, after putting in his garden, and arrived in New York in the middle of a snow storm. Not only was he out of place in the North in the snow, but he also felt out of place as a Southerner asking his recent enemy for money.

After several days, though, he was invited to preach at a church in Brooklyn and was warmly introduced by the rector. As Anthony stepped into the pulpit and began to speak, many of the parishioners stood up and eased themselves out of their pews to leave in protest. The aisles were crowded with people headed to the back of the church.

Suddenly a voice boomed from behind the pulpit. "Sexton, shut those doors!" The rector stood up and, glaring at his congregation, compelled them to return to their seats and listen. He didn't give them much choice because the sexton promptly locked the doors.

Not the way I had hoped to begin this morning. This congregation looks about as happy to be here as I used to be in Mr. Cotes' school. How to get them to listen?

Anthony resumed his sermon, but he added something he hadn't planned. Looking out over the angry faces in front of him, he said, "I don't want to speak to you with any false impression. I was a supporter of the Confederate cause, and did all I could do to be a minister of the Gospel of peace in the midst of the war. But once the war ended, and we laid down our arms, I, like many of my friends, did so in good faith. All wise men among us are making not only the most, but the best, of our condition." He could feel the shift in the congregation. Slowly the scowls disappeared; the arms unfolded. By the end of the service, Anthony had over one thousand dollars in the collection plate for his school for the freed slaves.

He found sympathetic listeners everywhere he preached. Northerners, like the ones in Brooklyn, at first were surprised and reluctant to listen to a minister from Charleston, the town notorious for firing the first shots of the Civil War. But once they heard that his intention was to improve the lives of the newly freed slaves by providing them an education, they listened with enthusiasm, gave him money to support his school, and sent him to other sympathetic congregations to explain his plans. With the support from the Northerners, and the endorsement of President Johnson to procure the federal Marine Hospital building for the school, Anthony opened a school for 1800 children of the former slaves in Charleston.

But once life in Charleston settled into a new normal, with a Northern principal and local teachers running the school, Anthony found time to visit Toomer's grave in Magnolia Cemetery almost every day. One beautiful, clear autumn morning with the birds singing in the trees overhead, Anthony knelt at his son's grave, lost in his thoughts of sadness and despair. No one else was around; he was alone with his grief. Suddenly, a voice came from the cloudless sky. "Stop grieving for the dead, and do something for the living."

Anthony looked around the cemetery. There was no one else there.

He spoke to the voice. "What can I do for the living?"

Again, the voice spoke. "Your child is enjoying what you are only hoping for; but see his young companions who are mostly poor orphans without church or school. Take them and educate them."

Anthony had successfully opened a school for the children of the former slaves; now he set his sights on a school for the young men whose education had been disrupted by the four long years of the war and by their poverty following the war.

Anthony thought about how he felt saving the fly from the spider the night before his home was auctioned. And about Mr. Dozier, who had saved their house for his family. He thought about his decision to study business instead of going on to college after prep school and about his business venture after the war to provide for his family. He thought about the generosity of the Northerners who wanted to support him in providing an education for black children in Charleston. Those experiences had prepared him for this undertaking.

He returned to the North, begged, borrowed, and called on friends for the means to open a school, and by March of 1868, with the funding in hand, he opened a school for thirty-three boarding students who arrived in Charleston from across South Carolina to begin their studies. Anthony remembered his own teachers— Miss Taylor, Mr. Prior, Mr. Cotes, and all the faculty at Mr. Zion—and was a firm, but kind, headmaster, who expected the best from his students. And at meals, he never counted spoonfuls of potatoes or butterbeans. Shortly after opening his boarding school, he admitted the young boys of Charleston as day students—many of whom had been orphaned by the war.

Each year—each day—the financial needs of the school weighed on Anthony's mind, but keeping in mind the spider and fly of his childhood and his promise in the graveyard, he resolved to do all he could to keep his school open. Each year, he made a visit to his friends in the North, who had been so helpful in supporting his school for the black children of Charleston. The Northern benefactors again, year after year, decade after decade, supplied what he needed to keep his school open.

Several times he went as far as England to preach and seek the funds to keep his school open, and found supporters in each place he traveled. Acts of Congress, introduced and supported by his former enemies such as General Sherman, and endorsed by several presidents, provided the buildings necessary to expand the school.

Anthony's desire to move past the war, to look forward, and to build connections between the black and white citizens of South Carolina and between the former enemies in the North and South led him to find sympathetic supporters. They helped him follow the voice he heard and keep alive the journey he undertook one autumn afternoon in Magnolia Cemetery as he knelt at his young son's grave.

Today a bronze statue of Anthony Toomer Porter stands on a pedestal between the middle and upper school buildings of Porter-Gaud School. Anthony's gaze takes in the daffodil-filled garden in front of him and the students who study—or hang out—on the low walls surrounding the green spaces between the school buildings. Frisbees

fly past his nose, students scurry by him on their way to the gym in the Wendell Center, birds soar above him to alight in the live oaks beside him, teachers stroll behind him discussing their latest project—or lunch.

The school he conceived of on that autumn afternoon still thrives, a testament to the dogged and patient work of the indomitable man in bronze.

About the Author

DEBORAH COE REINHOLD, an educator for almost five decades, taught in Vermont, Delaware, North Carolina, and South Carolina, spending the last twenty-five years at Porter-Gaud in Charleston. Beginning her writing career in retirement, she published *Southern Steel* in 2024.

Deborah lives with her husband Bob and their rescue dogs in Mount Pleasant, S.C.

www.ingramcontent.com/pod-product-compliance
Lightning Source LLC
Chambersburg PA
CBHW051322120626
46547CB00015B/2348